How to Probate an Estate

- A Step-By-Step Guide for Executors

enodare

by enodare publishing

Bibliographic data

- International Standard Book Number (ISBN): 978-1-906144-30-2
- Printed in the United States of America
- First Printing: January 2011

Published by: Enodare Limited
Unit 102
The Northumberlands
Lower Mount Street
Dublin 2
Ireland

Printed and distributed by: CreateSpace - An Amazon Company,
On-Demand Publishing LLC
Scotts Valley, CA 95066
United States of America

For more information, e-mail books@enodare.com.

Warning and disclaimer

Although precautions have been taken in the preparation of this book, neither the publisher nor the author assumes any responsibility for errors or omissions. No warranty of fitness is implied. The information is provided on an "as is" basis. The author and the publisher shall have neither liability nor responsibility to any person or entity with respect to any loss or damages (whether arising by negligence or otherwise) arising from the use of or reliance on the information contained in this book or from the use of any forms accompanying it.

IMPORTANT NOTE

This book is meant as a general guide to probating an estate. While considerable effort has been made to make this book as complete and accurate as possible, laws and their interpretation are constantly changing. As such, you are advised to update this information with your own research and/or counsel and to consult with your personal legal, financial and medical advisors before acting on any information contained in this book.

The purpose of this book is to educate and entertain. It is not meant to provide legal, financial or medical advice or to create any attorney-client or advisory relationship. The authors and publisher shall have neither liability (whether in negligence or otherwise) nor responsibility to any person or entity with respect to any loss or damage caused or alleged to be caused directly or indirectly by the information or documents contained in this book or the use of that information or those documents.

ABOUT ENODARE

Enodare, the international self-help legal publisher, was founded in 2000 by lawyers from one of the most prestigious international law firms in the World.

Our aim was simple - to provide access to quality legal information and products at an affordable price.

Our Will Writer software was first published in that year and, following its adaptation to cater for the legal systems of over 30 countries worldwide, quickly drew in excess of 40,000 visitors per month to our website. From this humble start, Enodare has quickly grown to become a leading international estate planning and asset protection self-help publisher with legal titles in the United States, Canada, the United Kingdom, Australia and Ireland.

Our publications provide customers with the confidence and knowledge to help them deal with everyday estate planning issues such as the preparation of a last will and testament, a living trust, a power of attorney, administering an estate and much more.

By providing customers with much needed information and forms, we enable them to place themselves in a position where they can protect both themselves and their families through the use of easy to read legal documents and forward planning techniques.

The Future....

We are always seeking to expand and improve the products and services we offer. However, in order to do this, we need to hear from interested authors and to receive feedback from our customers.

If something isn't clear to you in our publications, please let us know and we'll try to make it clearer in the next edition. If you can't find the answer you want and have a suggestion for an addition to our range, we'll happily look at that too.

enodare

USING SELF-HELP BOOKS

Before using a self-help book, you need to carefully consider the advantages and disadvantages of doing so – particularly where the subject matter is of a legal or tax related nature.

In writing our self-help books, we try to provide readers with an overview of the laws in a specific area. While this overview is often general in nature, it provides a good starting point for those wishing to carry out a more detailed review of a topic.

However, unlike an attorney advising a client, we cannot cover every conceivable eventuality that might affect our readers. Within the intended scope of this book, we can only cover the principal areas in a given topic and even where we cover these areas, we can still only to so to a moderate extent. To do otherwise would result in the writing of a text book which would be capable of use by legal professionals. This is not what we do.

We try to present useful information and documents that can be used by an average reader with little or no legal knowledge. While our sample documents can be used in the vast majority of cases, everybody's personal circumstances are different. As such, they may not be suitable for everyone. You may have personal circumstances which might impact the effectiveness of these documents or even your desire to use them. The reality is that without engaging an attorney to review your personal circumstances, this risk will always exist. It's for this very reason that you need to consider whether the cost of using a do-it-yourself legal document outweighs the risk that there may be something special about your particular circumstances which might not be taken into account by the sample documents attached to or referred to in this book (or indeed any other sample documents).

It goes without saying (we hope) that if you are in any doubt as to whether the documents in this book are suitable for use in your particular circumstances, you should contact a suitably qualified attorney for advice before using them. Remember the decision to use these documents is yours! We are not advising you in any respect.

In using this book, you should also take into account the fact that this book has been written with the purpose of providing a general overview of the laws in the United States. As such, it does not attempt to cover all of the various procedural nuances and specific requirements that may apply from state to state – although we do point some of these out along the way. Rather, in our book, we try to provide forms which give a fair example of the type of forms which are commonly used in most states. Nevertheless, it remains possible that your state may have specific requirements which have not been taken into account in our forms.

Another thing that you should remember is that the law changes – thousands of new laws are brought into force every day and, by the same token, thousands are repealed or amended every day! As such, it is possible that while you are reading this book, the law might well have been changed. Let's hope it hasn't but the chance does exist! Needless to say, we take regular steps (including e-mail alerts) to update our customers about any changes to the law. We also ensure that our books are reviewed and revised regularly to take account of these changes.

Anyway, assuming that all of the above is acceptable to you, let's move on to exploring the topic at hand..............probating an estate!

TABLE OF CONTENTS

AN INTRODUCTION TO PROBATE

Probating an estate requires a lot more from an executor than simply writing checks and handing over the assets of a deceased person to his or her named beneficiaries. It can be a demanding and time consuming task involving complicated taxes, fee payments, disputes amongst beneficiaries and tricky asset transfers. It's therefore important that you are properly prepared for the task before embarking on it. This preparation can take the form of reading one or more books, such as this one, as well as engaging the services of an experienced estate planning or probate attorney to assist you in navigating this sometimes difficult process.

Probate, in short, is a court supervised process by which a deceased person's property is transferred to the beneficiaries named in the deceased's will. If the deceased person has not made a will, this process will be known as an administration rather than a probate.

Every state has its own set of probate laws (often referred to as the probate code) which set out the specific rules and procedures for probate in that state. These laws typically set out the requirements for a will to be deemed validly made, tell us who is in charge of the deceased's estate after he or she dies, who is entitled to receive assets from that estate in circumstances where the deceased has or has not made a valid will, which creditors need to be paid upon the deceased's death and in what order of priority, how to distribute assets after the payment of taxes without breaching the law and so on.

While an attorney is not required to assist you with the probate process, the right probate attorney could help you maintain control over the costs associated with winding up the estate thereby ensuring that they are kept to a minimum. A good attorney could also save you countless hours of work and relieve you of much of the stress that emanates from the probate process.

However, an executor's role is often not a complex one. As such, with proper preparation on your part, there should be no reason why you cannot conduct much of the process yourself.

The probate process can often be relatively straight forward and routine. At the outset, you will need to locate a copy of the deceased's will and prove to the probate court that it is in fact the last will of the deceased and, more importantly, that it is valid. This process usually involves the presentation of the will to the court and the production of simple affidavits from the people who witnessed the deceased signing the will. Once the court confirms the validity of the will, you can be appointed as the executor or personal representative of the estate of the deceased (provided of course you are named as such in the will); and will be responsible for the location, collection and distribution of the deceased's assets.

Once you have had the assets of the deceased's estate collected and valued and have determined the level of debt owing by the estate, you will be able to determine whether the net value of the deceased's estate is small enough to undergo the simplified probate procedures which exist in many states (we'll cover this in more detail in later chapters) and whether any income and estate death taxes are owed by the estate. You will also be able to commence the payment of any bills owed by the deceased at the time of death.

Once all matters concerning the estate have been resolved, you can distribute the assets of the estate to the named beneficiaries and close off probate. When this is done, you simply file appropriate records with the court and that's it – job done!

The entire process can be long and often takes up to 12 months to complete. Of course, if complications arise this process may end up dragging on for years! For this reason, you should always consider contacting an attorney if something unexpected occurs during the probate process. This may end up saving the estate unnecessary costs and delays; not to mention saving you hours of work!

This book is designed to guide you step-by-step through the probate process and to give you the knowledge and confidence to act as an executor if you are asked — or even to offer to take on the role. On the other hand, if you reach the end of this book and still feel disinclined to take on the job of executor — you will have a fund of knowledge which will enable you to discuss the subject intelligently with other people.

CHAPTER 1:
OVERVIEW OF PROBATE AND THE EXECUTOR'S ROLE

Chapter Overview

In this chapter, we'll take a brief look at the probate process and the role of the executor generally. This will give you a good insight into what executors do.

CHAPTER 1

OVERVIEW OF PROBATE AND THE EXECUTOR'S ROLE

What Is Probate and How Is it Commenced?

Probate has come to mean not just proving the validity of a last will and testament but the entire administrative process involving the collecting of assets, payment of debts and the passing of a deceased person's legal title to property to his or her beneficiaries.

The person responsible for carrying out this administrative process is called an executor or a legal representative.

Because a will is required for probate, one of the first tasks facing you as executor will be to locate the will. Not only does the will tell you how the deceased wished to distribute his or her estate but it will also allow you to confirm that you have in fact been appointed as executor of the deceased's estate. Once you find the will, you will need to determine whether it is indeed a valid will on its face, ensuring for example that it has been signed by the testator and witnessed by the correct number of witnesses. Most states require that a will be witnessed by two witnesses (in Vermont, you must have three witnesses).

The next step is for you to confirm that this is in fact the last will of the deceased, as generally only the last will has legal effect (new wills tend to revoke old wills in their entirety). This is why it's important that a testator physically destroys any pre-existing wills and codicils when he or she makes a new will. At least, in that way, where can be no room for argument as to which will is in fact the testator's last will.

Assuming that the will appears in order, you will then need to determine whether probate is required and, if so, apply for your letters of authority.

Letters of Authority

'Letters of authority' (or 'letters testamentary' as it is also called) is the name given to the document issued by the probate court appointing an executor to commence probate of a deceased person's estate. If the deceased failed to make a will, the letters issued will be called 'letters of administration' instead. Letters of administration authorize a person to administrator the estate of a deceased person in accordance with state intestacy laws.

There are there different types of letters that can be issued by the probate court. These include:

1. <u>Letters of authority</u>
   Letters of authority are issued where one or more executors have been appointed under the terms of a deceased's last will and testament. The letters authorize the named executor to administer the estate in accordance with the terms of the deceased's will.

2. <u>Letters of administration (with will annexed)</u>
   These letters are issued when the deceased has in fact made a will but has either failed to nominate an executor or the executor that has been nominated is unable or unwilling to carry out the probate proceedings.

3. <u>Letters of administration</u>
   Letters of administration are issued when the deceased has either not made a will or, where a will has been made, the will turns out to be invalid.

Did You Know?

Where no will has been made the person charged with winding up the deceased's estate will be known as an administrator.

Each of the letters allows the person named therein to represent the deceased's estate for the purpose of winding it up. In the majority of cases, the issuing of letters is merely an administrative process. However, before a prospective executor applies for letters it's important that he or she understands the importance of the letters and whether same are in fact needed! We'll have a look at this in the ensuing pages.

Why Are Letters of Authority Necessary?

Organizations such as banks and insurance companies (and indeed others) which hold money in the deceased's name need to know to whom that money should be paid following the death of the original account/policy holder. As the letters have been issued by the court, it amounts to proof for the lending institutions and insurance companies that the person named in the letters is legally entitled to collect in and distribute the assets of the deceased account/policy holder. This, in turn, allows these types of institutions to legally pay the monies they hold to the executor/administrator named in the letters and that payment amounts to good discharge on their behalf. After that, the distribution of the estate to the correct people is the responsibility of the person named as executor in the letters.

These states use the term "personal representative" instead of "executor"		
Alaska	Maine	North Dakota
Arizona	Michigan	South Carolina
Colorado	Minnesota	South Dakota
Florida	Montana	Utah
Hawaii	Nebraska	Wisconsin
Idaho	New Mexico	

Are Letters of Authority Always Needed?

Letters of authority may not be needed where the estate amounts to a "small estate" or in respect of any of the deceased's assets which do not need to go through probate. We will discuss each of these in later chapters.

In addition, organizations will sometimes agree to release monies without the production of letters of authority. They may however attach specific conditions to the release of the funds. Nonetheless, where the holding is small, it may be worth investigating whether the organization in question would release the money in the absence of having the letters of authority.

When it comes to assets with formal legal titles such as real property or stocks, if the legal title to the asset vests solely in the name of the deceased (i.e. excluding jointly held assets), the executor must obtain letters of authority in order to enable him or her to formally transfer or sell that asset.

Important Note

If you are in any doubt as to what type of letters are required or whether letters of authority are required at all, speak to your lawyer.

Who Is Entitled to Apply for Letters of Authority/ Administration?

There are some basic rules of priority which determine who may apply for a letter of authority. While these rules of priority can vary from case to case and from state to state, they can generally be put in the following order:-

- person named as executor or alternate executor in a will;
- surviving spouse (or their nominee);
- other beneficiaries under the will (or their nominee);
- heirs-at-law (non-beneficiaries) (or their nominee); and
- creditors.

The Executor's Role Once Appointed

Once a petition for probate has been made it's then the probate court's job to formally rule upon the validity of the deceased's will (quite often this is just a rubber-stamp affair). Any challengers to the will (or part thereof) must file their objection within a specified amount of time (this time frame changes from state to state, so you will need to check the requirements for your particular state).

If the court deems the will valid and accepts your appointment as executor, it will issue letters of authority. Once these letters have issued, you may then begin to pay taxes, settle debts with creditors and other claims against the deceased's estate and then distribute the assets to the beneficiaries named in the will. If, for some reason, the will is found to be invalid you will need to proceed as if the deceased had died intestate. In which case, the court will appoint an administrator to administer the estate. This may or may not be you depending on the laws of the state in which the deceased was resident.

Finally, the last step of the process occurs when you finalize the estate by filing the necessary papers and accounts with the court. These must include an accounting of assets that formed part of the estate; details of what was paid out from the estate (and why); copies of any notices and tax returns issued, received or filed in connection with the estate. You will be expected to provide proof of distribution of the deceased's assets to the correct beneficiaries, usually by providing signed receipts from the beneficiaries. Also included may be copies of deeds (signed by you as executor) for the transfer of real property and instruments of distribution for any of the deceased's personal property.

As soon as the court recognizes that you have successfully completed all steps necessary to administer the deceased's estate, you will be released from further service as executor. The same would apply to a court appointed administrator as well.

Important Note

Remember, as executor, you can retain probate lawyers to deal with most if not all of the above items on your behalf. The fees payable for the service of this lawyer will be borne by the estate of the deceased and not by you, the executor, personally!!

Who Is Entitled to Be an Executor?

Usually, the person or people named as executors under the deceased's last will and testament will be appointed as executors of the deceased's will. In many cases, this will be a spouse, relative or close friend of the deceased. In other cases, the deceased may have chosen to appoint a lawyer or bank as executor. In practice, a person making a will is relatively free to decide who to appoint as executor. There are however some legal restrictions.

Certain states impose restrictions on who can act as an executor. Normally, a person will not be able to act as an executor if they are under the age of majority in their state, have been convicted of a felony or are not a U.S. citizen.

Out-of-State Executors

Complications can also arise where someone living outside the deceased's state of residence is named as an executor. While the majority of sates allow people to appoint executors who are living in a different state, many states require that this person be a relative or a primary beneficiary under the testator's will. Other states require a non-resident executor to post a bond to ensure that the beneficiaries under the will are protected against potential wrongdoings by the executor. While in some jurisdictions, the terms of a will can specifically waive the posting of such a bond, others disallow this and the costs of these bonds can be expensive.

Did You Know?

A testator is the name given to a person who makes a will. Originally, the term testator only included male will makers. The term testatrix was used when referring to a female will maker. However, with the advent of time, the word testator now commonly includes both male and female will makers.

How Long Does Probate Take?

The time it takes to probate an estate will ultimately depend on the assets and liabilities of the deceased and whether or not his or her affairs were in order at the time of death. If the deceased's estate was complicated, it may take a considerable period of time to determine precisely what assets were held and debts owed by the deceased; and thereafter to discharge any debts and taxes. Alternatively, there may be difficulties locating beneficiaries or even legal challenges to the legality of the will or even specific provisions of the will. Each of these events is likely to cause a delay in the probate process should they occur.

Each state has its own set of procedures for probate and these will need to be complied with. Some states even have procedures for 'small estates' which can speed up the probate process. Taking all of these factors into account, probate can take anywhere from 3 to 6 months to a number of years. By way of simple example, the average time for the probate process in California is 7 to 9 months, if all goes well. Of course, if there is a legal challenge to the will or some other lawsuit, this time can be substantially increased. There are many probates which have been ongoing for decades!

Generally speaking, however, probate should be completed within one year. This period of time is known as the 'executor's year'. If, for whatever reason, probate has not been completed within that time frame, the executor may be required to file a status report with the probate court to provide an explanation of what still has to be done to complete probate and an estimate of how much time it's likely to take.

In the event that the executor fails to report, the beneficiaries under a will can ask the court to make an order requiring the filing of such a report and/or can take any other action they deem necessary to close probate including the removal of the personal representative and the appointment of someone else in their stead.

How Much Will Probate Cost?

The cost of probate differs from place to place and is generally determined by either state law or custom and practice in a particular area. When all the costs associated with probate are added up probate can easily cost from 1% to 7% (or even more) of the value of an estate. As some of these probate costs are set by state law there is very little that you can do to mitigate or reduce them (other than avoid probate of course!).

Certain states, such as California, for example, prescribe for maximum fees which a lawyer can charge for probating an estate. These maximum fees are based on the gross value of the estate. By gross value, we mean the total value of the estate before any debts or liabilities are subtracted from the estate. As such, these fees can be quite high. Consider for example a case where the principal asset of the estate was a property worth $1 million with a mortgage of $900,000 secured against that property. Notwithstanding that the net realizable value of the asset on a sale is only $100,000, the attorney will be able to charge fees based on a percentage of $1 million. If the legal fee is say 5%, this will result in legal fees of $50,000 for something with a net value of $100,000!!!

Needless to say, if someone contests the will or if there is any other litigation in respect of the assets of the estate, there is no way to determine by how much these costs could rise.

The table below, which is based on the California probate code, will give you a good idea of likely statutory probate costs. These represent the maximum amounts which a lawyer can charge (assuming that there are no unusual taxes or legal issues associated with the probate).

Estate Value	Statutory Fee
$100,000	$4,000
$200,000	$7,000
$300,000	$9,000
$400,000	$11,000
$500,000	$13,000

Estate Value	Statutory Fee
$600,000	$15,000
$700,000	$17,000
$800,000	$19,000
$900,000	$21,000
$1,000,000	$23,000
$2,000,000	$33,000

In New York, probate fees are payable at the rate of 5% on the first $100,000 of the estate, 4% on the next $200,000, 3% on the next $700,000, 2.5% on the next $4 million and 2% on the rest.

You should check the amount of probate fees chargeable in your state.

Do You Need a Lawyer?

Well, the simple answer to this question is no! If the estate of the deceased is not overly complex and you are prepared to do some research as well as put in the time and effort necessary to probate the estate, then you should be able to complete the probate on your own accord. In fact, many people actually probate estates without engaging a lawyer. A large number also engage lawyers merely to watch over their shoulder as they go through the process.

However, because one little mistake could set an executor back months, the vast majority of people tend to engage lawyers for the purpose of assisting them with the probate process. An experienced lawyer will immediately know what needs to be done to probate an estate, will have come across pretty much every conceivable problem that could arise in the probate process and will be able to ensure that all the boxes are ticked and that there will be no unnecessary delays in the process arising from the executor's inexperience.

If having read this book and done all the necessary research, you feel confident enough to take on the process alone, you are perfectly free to do so. However, if you are in any doubt as to what needs to be done, whether before or during the process, we recommend that you contact a lawyer. A wrong decision or a misunderstanding on your part could cause major delays in the process, as well as exposing you to actions for negligence if the wrongdoing on your part causes a loss to the estate.

As such, while it's not necessary to engage a lawyer, it can often be very beneficial in terms of ensuring a smooth and quick winding up of the estate and protecting you from allegations and claims of wrongdoings.

The final decision is of course yours to make!

CHAPTER 2:
DUTIES AND RESPONSIBILITIES OF EXECUTORS

Chapter Overview

In this chapter, we will give you an idea of some of the main duties, responsibilities and liabilities facing executors. These should all be taken into consideration before deciding whether to accept the role.

CHAPTER 2

DUTIES AND RESPONSIBILITIES OF EXECUTORS

Important Note

You should carefully contemplate all factors involved before deciding whether or not to take on the role of executor. Don't simply accept the role out of a sense of obligation. You must be both comfortable with and willing to perform the tasks associated with appointment!

Responsibilities of an Executor

An executor is responsible for managing the estate of a deceased person in accordance with the probate rules and procedures of the state where the probate takes place. We talked about some of the main responsibilities in Chapter 1, but be aware that, in particular cases, there may be various others.

A summary of the executor's main responsibilities include the flowing tasks:

- locating the will;
- checking its validity;
- filing an application for probate in the probate court registry. If the estate is worth less than a certain amount (dependent on state law) formal probate may not be required;

- notifying beneficiaries listed in the will that you have filled for probate;
- drafting and arranging publication of a notice of the deceased's death and sending a copy of the notice (by mail) to each creditor that the executor knows of;
- sending copies of the deceased's official death notice to the post office, utility companies, banks and credit card companies;
- collecting, securing and inventorying assets; and then having them appraised and valued;
- collecting all moneys owing to the estate;
- if the deceased was employed, checking with his/her employer for any unpaid salary or benefits;
- filing for outstanding social security, civil service, veteran and other benefits;
- filing claims for life insurance benefits;
- filing state death tax and federal estate tax returns;
- paying out valid and proven claims against the estate;
- distributing all remaining assets to the beneficiaries;
- filing all relevant papers with the probate court to wind up the estate; and
- closing probate.

Did You Know?

A person acting as an executor will be subject to certain laws, regulations, standards and guidelines including (amongst others):

- the terms of the last will and testament;
- the law of trusts which is a body of principles adopted by courts over the years which apply to executors and trustees;
- state & federal laws; and
- regulations.

General Duties of an Executor

As an executor, you will have a general duty to administer the deceased's estate and to distribute the estate to the beneficiaries named under the deceased's will or, in the absence of a will, to the deceased's heirs in accordance with state intestacy laws. In carrying out this duty, you will be obliged to act promptly and in the best interests of both the estate and the deceased's beneficiaries or, as the case may be, heirs.

You will also have a number of other duties, including the following:

- to take possession of the deceased's property;
- to manage, protect and preserve the estate;
- to prepare an inventory of all the probatable assets and property owned by the deceased at the time of death. This inventory should be prepared within a specific time frame, usually three months of the executor's appointment. The inventory should list each item of property together with its market value at the date of death of the deceased, as well as set

out details of any encumbrances registered against the asset in question. Where market valuations have been carried out, details of the valuation agent used should also be included;

- to publish a creditor's notice in a newspaper circulating in the county in which probate is filed once a week for three successive weeks. The notice should stipulate that the deceased has died, provide details of your appointment as executor and state that creditors of the deceased's estate can present details of any claims they might have against the estate for a period of three months following the date of first publication. Once this period of time expires, creditors will no longer be able to take a claim against the estate;

- to decide which creditors' claims should be allowed and which should be disallowed; and

- to pay allowed creditors' claims in the following order:

  (i) funeral expenses;

  (ii) costs and expenses associated with the administration of the estate;

  (iii) federal debts and taxes owed by the estate;

  (iv) medical expenses associated with the final illness of the deceased;

  (v) state debts and taxes owed by the estate; and

  (vi) all other claims.

Did You Know?

Duty to prepare an inventory of the deceased's assets

The Probate Code requires that, three months after his or her appointment, an executor must prepare an inventory of property owned by the deceased at the time of death, listing it with reasonable detail, and indicating as to each listed item, its fair market value as of the date of the deceased's death, and the type and amount of any encumbrance that may exist with reference to any item. The executor is obliged to send a copy of the inventory to all interested persons who request it and/or file the original of the inventory with the court (in which case it goes on the public record).

Fiduciary Duties of an Executor

A fiduciary relationship is a relationship which implies a position of trust or confidence in which one person is entrusted to hold or manage property or money on behalf of another.

Did You Know?

A fiduciary is someone who has undertaken to act for and on behalf of another in a particular matter in circumstances which give rise to a relationship of trust and confidence.

As a fiduciary, the executor owes a number of duties to the testator and to the beneficiaries of the testator's estate. These duties include duties to:-

- adhere to the terms of the will;

- locate, take possession and secure the estate assets;
- keep estate assets separate from other assets;
- keep accurate records and accounts of the estate's dealings;
- provide information to the beneficiaries named under the will in a timely manner;
- administer the estate with the same due care and skill that a person of ordinary prudence would exercise in dealing with his or her own property;
- administer the estate in the best interests of the beneficiaries; and
- avoid conflicts of interest.

Duty to Adhere to the Terms of the Will

While this may appear to be a very obvious statement, it is surprising how often executors' decisions are made without referring back to the provisions of the will to establish whether the act in question is permitted under the terms of the will. A prudent executor should always commence their role by carefully reading the terms of the will in order to understand the scope of the duties assigned to them and to determine what immediate actions he or she must take.

Duty to Secure Assets

An executor should immediately locate and secure all of the assets owned by the testator. If real estate or other valuables need to be insured or secured for a period of time, this needs to be arranged.

Duty to Keep Estate Assets Separate from Other Assets

The executor should ensure that the estate assets are kept wholly separate from his or her own and that the title to each of the estate assets rest with the estate and not personally with the executor. The executor must account in full for all income generated by the estate and should not borrow or otherwise take money from the estate for his or her personal interest.

Duty to Act Personally

Unless the terms of the will permit, executors must act personally and may not delegate the performance of tasks or the making of decisions concerning the deceased's estate – although the executor is normally permitted to take legal and other professional advice where he or she deems it appropriate.

Duty to Act in the Best Interests of the Beneficiaries

The executor is required to act impartially and in the best interests of the estate's beneficiaries.

Duty to Account

The executor has the responsibility of keeping detailed records of the estate and for providing an accounting to the beneficiary or beneficiaries under the will. The executor must keep detailed records of income generated by the estate's assets, any sale or purchase of estate assets and any payments made from the estate including taxes and distributions.

Duty to Invest Prudently

State law generally provides that an executor is required to exercise the due care, diligence and skill that a prudent person would exercise in managing the affairs of the estate. It therefore should go without saying that an executor needs to diversify the estate's investments in order to balance risk. However, in tandem with doing this, the executor also needs to ensure the generation of income from the estate assets as well as ensuring the future growth of those assets. As a result, it often makes sense for an executor (who, to be fair, often does not have a huge degree of investment experience) to engage the services of an investment advisor who can provide guidance to the executor in the investment process. Remember, if the executor fails to act diligently and prudently, he or she could find themselves at the back end of a law suit by the beneficiaries if there is a depletion in the value of the estate assets. However, if the executor acts prudently, he or she will substantially reduce the risk of personal liability.

Important Note

Certain state laws, such as those in Washington, require executors to exercise the same "judgment and care" that a person of ordinary prudence and intelligence would exercise in managing his or her own affairs. This does not however mean that an executor can take the same risks with the estate assets as he or she would with their own assets. On the contrary, it means that executors have to be even more prudent when dealing with estate assets.

Duty to Carry Out Duties Without Payment

Save in respect of out-of-pocket expenses and the payment of reasonable compensation, executors are generally required to act without payment unless the terms of the will provide otherwise. Professional executors will always ensure that a power to pay them is contained in the will's provisions before they act.

Duty to Not Benefit Personally

As a fiduciary, an executor may not benefit himself or herself personally unless the will specifically allows for this. Executors are required to act in good faith and to avoid conflicts of interest. When a conflict of interest arises, an executor should act carefully and consider taking professional advice.

Even good intentions are not an acceptable excuse for breaching this duty. For example, let's assume you were an executor of an estate which had a vast amount of real estate but very little cash available to pay debts and taxes. Even where you think it might be beneficial to purchase a piece of real estate at fair value from the estate to help cash flows, this could well be conceived as "self-dealing" and a presumption would be raised that you have a conflict of interest. This could lead the beneficiaries of the estate to challenge your actions in court.

As such, its best avoid these circumstances…or at least obtain the consent of the beneficiaries to the dealings in advance.

Of course, simply agreeing to act as an executor does not mean that you cannot engage professionals such as attorneys, accountants and financial advisors to assist you in the process of carrying out your duties and responsibilities. By engaging professionals when needed and by carrying out your duties with due care and attention, you will substantially reduce the risk of breaching your fiduciary duties.

Important Note

Remember, chose your professional advisors with care! Here are some simple questions that you may wish to ask your advisor before formally engaging them:-

- What licenses, certificates and registrations do you hold?
- What services do you provide?
- What type of clients do you work for?
- How many clients do you have?
- How long have you been in this business?
- What are your educational credentials?
- What is your specific field of expertise?
- How do you keep up to date with changes in your field?
- What professional references can you give me?
- Is your performance record verified by independent sources?
- How are your fees calculated?

Important Note

- Do you have a minimum account fee?
- What exact services will I receive for that fee?
- How often do you communicate with your clients?

Powers of an Executor

Until termination of his or her appointment, an executor has the same power over the title to property of the deceased's estate that an absolute owner would have. However, this power is exercisable in trust for the benefit of the creditors and others interested in the deceased's estate. This power may be exercised without notice, hearing or order of court.

In addition, executors are afforded a variety of additional powers under state law. These include powers to:

- employ persons for the purpose of valuing assets and evaluating the liabilities of the estate;
- receive a defined level of compensation or a reasonable level of compensation in return for acting as executor of the estate;
- petition the court for an order determining the validity of a will, the entitlement of beneficiaries to claim under the will, the entitlement of heirs to claim from the estate in the absence of a will, approving the final accounting of the estate as prepared by the executor and the plan of distribution of the estate assets; and
- close the probate or administration of the estate.

In addition to the powers granted under state law, executors tend to be afforded further powers under the terms of a will. These additional powers are given to the executor to allow him manage the deceased's estate. Typically, the larger the estate the greater the extent of the powers given to executors. For instance, if the deceased has a large property portfolio and a variety of business interests, he or she may need to give wide management powers or even a power of sale to the executor in order to ensure that the value of these assets can be maintained for the benefit of the beneficiaries.

Executor's Liability

There are numerous risks that come with being appointed as an executor. We have set out below some examples (but not an exhaustive list) of ways in which an executor may be held liable for a breach of duty or responsibility.

- An executor can be held liable if he or she:-
  - violates any applicable law;
  - fails to comply with the terms of the will;
  - abuses any of his or her powers as executor; or
  - deals in the estate assets for his or her own account.

- The administration of the estate generally needs to be commenced and concluded within a reasonable period of time. If the executor fails to do this and, as a result, the beneficiaries under the will are exposed to any form of financial or pecuniary loss, he or she could be held liable for the loss.

- An executor, is obliged to secure and protect the assets of the estate. If he or she fails to do this and it results in the assets being damaged, lost or stolen then (in the absence of having adequate insurance over the assets covering the loss) he or she could be held personally liable for the loss or, as the case may be, the reduction in the value of the assets in question. Similarly, if the executor fails to properly manage, insure or repair real property (whether commercial or residential) he or she could be held liable for any losses including loss of rental income.

- Executors are required to act prudently in the management of estate assets and investments. If an executor acts without due care and prudence, such as in the case of buying speculative securities or disposing of valuable assets substantially below market value, he or she could be held accountable.

- While executors can take professional advice before making investment decisions, the ability to make these decisions is personal to the executor and cannot be delegated. Therefore any improper delegation of executor duties, such as allowing investment advisors complete scope to make decisions in respect of and deal with the estate's investments without executor supervision, could result in liability being imposed on the executor. The same principle applies irrespective of the assets in question. As such, it would apply equally to allowing someone to freely manage the deceased's business or property portfolio etc. If an executor engages a professional to manage some aspect of the estate, the executor most closely supervise the carrying out of those management functions – it is his or her responsibility after all!

- An executor, is responsible for ensuring that the correct people benefit from the estate. If the executor accidently makes payments or distributions to the wrong people, he or she could be held personally liable to make good the damage caused by securing the return of the misplaced assets or compensating the beneficiaries accordingly.

- Taking actions without the proper approval can also expose executors to liability. Depending on the proposed action in question, an executor may require the prior consent of beneficiaries, co-fiduciaries or even a court!

- An executor will always need to ensure that he or she has properly attended to the payment of all creditor accounts, including any taxation liabilities. An executor will be personally liable to ensure these payments are made.

It should be borne in mind that a beneficiary named under the terms of a testator's will or even a co-executor can institute legal proceedings against the executor for breach of duty/responsibility. The remedies that can be sought by the litigant vary depending on the nature of the alleged breach of duty/responsibility and the specific circumstances involved. However, the principal remedies available would include an order of court:

- compelling the executor to perform his or her duties;
- preventing the executor from committing a potential violation of his or her duties;
- requiring the executor to compensate the estate for the violation;
- removing the executor; and/or
- disqualifying the executor from ever acting as an executor again.

As alluded to above, where an executor is found guilty of a breach of his or her duties or responsibilities the court can require the executor to compensate the estate for the amount of any loss suffered by it. The compensation amount is often referred to as a "surcharge".

Important Note

If you are in any doubt as to your specific duties as executor or if you are concerned as to whether a particular course of action might lead to a breach of duty, we recommend that you seek the advice of an attorney.

Protections for the Executor from Liability

There are a number of ways that you, as executor, can be protected from liability. This protection may be against malfeasance (a term that refers to the committing of an illegal act, especially by a public official) or negligence. While some of these methods need to be provided for under the terms of a will, others can be implemented after the testator's death.

Protection Under the Terms of a Will

The terms of a will can be drafted in a manner so as to reduce the chance of an executor being exposed to personal liability in circumstances where he or she acts diligently and in good faith in the carrying out of his or her duties. By way of simple example, a will could authorize an executor to manage a particular business activity that was somewhat risky and, in conjunction with doing that, could provide that the executor will not be held liable for any loss to the value of that business where he or she acts in good faith. The rationale for the inclusion of such clauses is relatively straight forward. In the absence of including these exclusion clauses, executors would abstain from taking on any involvement in the management of such assets in circumstances where they could find themselves being sued personally for any subsequent loss – even where they did all they could humanly do! These clauses allow executors to get on with the business at hand while at the same time ensuring that they still act with due care and attention in the performance of their duties.

Obtain the Consent of Beneficiaries

Another way in which an executor can reduce the possibility of personal liability is to obtain the written permission of all concerned beneficiaries before taking a particular course of action or carrying out certain activities, for example the sale of real estate investments. While it's not vital, the written consent should expressly state that the beneficiaries will not hold the executor liable if they carry out the approved action(s). The mere existence of such a written approval would make it exceptionally difficult for beneficiaries to subsequently take a successful action against the executor for losses to the estate incurred from the carrying out of the approved activities (unless of course the executor was negligent in carrying out the activities approved by the beneficiaries).

Take Out an Executor's Insurance Bond

One of the best protections available to executors in the current market is insurance cover. The estate and/or the executor can take out executor insurance in the form of a surety bond, obtainable from most insurance companies. The bond protects both beneficiaries and creditors from losses suffered by the estate due to neglect or omission by the executor. Although a bond is not always required, beneficiaries may request it (simply if they feel it is necessary) and even the probate court might request it from time to time. Needless to say, while it protects the estate, it also protects the executor from personal liability as he is afforded monetary protection up to the value of the insurance bond. The value of the bond should, in most cases, equate to the full value of the estate. The premium for the bond will be payable by the estate.

Obtain the Consent of the Probate Court

Finally, where an executor is uncertain as to how to proceed in a particular situation, he or she may apply to court for directions on how to proceed. Having considered the issue, the court will direct the executor on how best to proceed in the circumstances. This direction will be given in the form of a court order. Where the executor follows the directions of the court order to the letter, it would be extremely difficult for a beneficiary to take action personally against the executor given that he or she is carrying out actions sanctioned by the court. Of course, if the court was not aware of all the facts in the case, the executor would not be adequately protected in this instance.

Payment of Compensation to Executors

Generally speaking, the amount of compensation payable to executors for carrying out their work ranges from between 2% to 4% of the value of the estate or, in many cases, is limited to 'reasonable compensation'. As the amount which an executor can receive is set out under state law, this amount varies from state to state and also tends to decrease on a percentage basis as the size of the estate increases.

Remember also that as many executors are often relatives or close friends of the deceased they do not charge for performing their duties as executor.

Executors are generally unable to recover either fees for the provision of their services or reimbursement for out-of-pocket expenses without the prior approval of the court. In circumstances where it materializes that the executor was incompetent or failed to carry out his or her duties and/or responsibilities as executor, the court may deny the payment of compensation to the executor or reduce the amount which ought to be payable to the executor.

Should You Accept the Role?

While it's an onerous obligation, the task of being an executor for a family member or a close friend can be seen as a final act of friendship. It's often humbling that someone trusts you sufficiently to invite you to accept this very personal responsibility. In many ways, you should feel honored to have been chosen.

However, having been chosen for this job is not of itself sufficient reason to accept the responsibility especially if you are not 100% committed to the task. In such circumstances, it's much better for everyone if you decline the job when you are originally asked, rather than for you to half-heartedly agree to act and then decide you can't do it after the testator's passing.

Assuming however that you're willing in principle at least to carry out the job, there's no reason to refuse to accept the position. Let's assume that you've been approached to become a friend's executor and feel you are competent enough, but are not quite sure what to do and when to do it. Well there's no need to panic, help is at hand! With the assistance of this book, we'll guide you step-by-step through each stage of the probate process from start to finish.

Even if you feel a bit out of your depth at any stage and feel it would be beneficial to the estate for you to do so, there's no reason why you should not seek the advice and assistance of an experienced professional — be it a lawyer, accountant or otherwise. Remember, you are entitled to seek professional assistance at the expense of the estate.

All that said, you may very well have good reason for your hesitancy in serving as executor, even for a close friend or family member's estate.

Are you in poor health generally? Or are you aware that there is a strong possibility of conflict between certain beneficiaries of the estate which you really don't want to be involved in? Possibly the deceased carried a lot of debt and this is another thing that concerns you? These sorts of things are valid reasons for you to hesitate about accepting or even to reject the role of executor.

If after taking all of the above into consideration you are still willing to take on the role, remember that the only qualities an executor really cannot do without are conscientiousness, integrity and common sense! Frankly, if you have an organized mind, are reasonably prudent and are detail oriented, there is absolutely no reason for you to have doubts about serving. Remember you can always seek help from a lawyer or accountant if in the end you find that you need to!

What to Expect When Appointed!

Don't expect all plain sailing when you agree to do the job! There are bound to be one or two delays and difficulties in the smoothest of estate administrations. The tardy debtor, the disputatious heir, the accidental or fraudulent claim for an account already paid (by the deceased), even the occasional difficulty in tracking down a beneficiary — at least one of these things will be sent to haunt most honest, hard-working executors!

Not to mention that these nagging difficulties will probably hold up the finalization of the estate. But eventually, all these hiccups are quelled and the executor can retire gracefully with a fund of "war stories" for future dinner parties.

All jokes aside, as an executor you really do need to ensure things keep moving, so the value of the estate does not suffer. As such, you need to be aware of the various stages involved in the probate process and what you will be required to do next. Be sure, therefore to carefully read this book form start to finish if you do accept the role!

Resigning After Accepting the Appointment

While you may have initially felt confident enough to take on the role of executor, you may subsequently discover that there is a lot more involved than you thought. You may even feel that the role is far to demanding both in terms of its time requirement and the strains caused by the complexity of the estate. You may even feel that you've taken on more than you can cope with.

The good news is that you don't have to complete the job even where you have given your prior agreement and/or have been approved by the court. However, there will be some procedural requirements that you must first deal with before vacating the position. Given that you took on the role of executor, you cannot simply walk away of your own accord. As a matter of law, once you commence acting as executor, or intermeddle in an estate as it's also called, you are responsible for the administration of the estate. As such, if you wish to resign as executor after taking control of the testator's property, you must formally renounce your position in writing. In order to do this, you will need to submit a letter of renunciation in writing to the probate court. The precise form of this letter can vary from state to state. As such, you should check with your local probate office to see what precise form is required.

You will also have to provide the court with any information you have already gathered in relation to the deceased's estate. This information will subsequently be passed on to the person who takes on the role of executor following your departure. If there was a second or alternate executor named in the will, this person will be asked to accept the role. If they are unwilling or unable to accept the role, the court will choose someone to act as executor in the same way as it would choose a person to act as an administrator if there was no will – see chapter 1.

Important Note

If you have decided to resign, remember to let the immediate relatives of the deceased know of your decision so that they can deal with the appointment of a new executor/administrator.

Declining to Act as Executor

While people chosen to be executor should always be asked prior to the event, the reality is that the task is sometimes sprung on the person completely out of the blue. If you have been appointed as executor and are unwilling to take on the role, you are free to decline to act at any time! By this we mean that you can not only say "no" when you are initially asked to act as executor, but you can also decide on the death of the testator that you do not want to take the job of executor on (even where you have previously agreed to accept the role and have been expressly nominated in the will). For instance, you may have come to the decision that it's just too much trouble and responsibility. And that's perfectly fine! It's only after the filing of the petition for probate in the probate court that your right to resign is restricted (see above).

An executor's job is often not an easy one, especially where the affairs of the deceased were not in order at the time of death and where the deceased owed a lot of debt or has insurance or employment benefits outstanding. Obviously, the more assets and liabilities that the deceased had the longer it will take to wind up their estate. These potential complications and delays alone are often enough to encourage would be executors to turn down the role.

Probate can be a long drawn out and demanding process even with the assistance of an experienced probate lawyer. If the estate is complex, you may not be comfortable with your ability to carry out your duties or may even be worried about potential exposure to liability. If, at the end of the day, you feel (for whatever reason) that you would be unable for the job, then you should not accept the position. This would undoubtedly be the best for everyone.

Remember however, even where you decline to act as executor you are legally required to file the deceased's will with the deceased's local probate office if you are in possession of it. There are specific time lines within which the will must be presented to the probate office – often within 30 days of discovery of same. You should check your state laws or with the local probate court to determine the precise requirements in this respect.

Sample Form

Sample Renunciation of Executorship – New Jersey

(When you are named in a will as the Executor but you do not wish to act, this form is used)

State of New Jersey Ocean County Surrogate's court

In the Matter of the Estate of

____________________________ , deceased.

Renunciation of Executorship:_______

To the Surrogate of the County of Ocean:
Whereas, Deceased, late of__________________________________ in the County of Ocean died on ___________________________ , leaving a Last Will dated _________________________ ,
and naming____ the Executor/rix thereof.

Now be it known that ____ ________ hereby renounces the said executorship and refuses to take upon himself/herself the burden of the same.

____

Signed in the presence of

____

Notary Public

STATE OF NEW JERSEY

COUNTY OF ss:

Be it Remembered, that on ______________________________ before me, the undersigned authority personally appeared ____________________________ _______ who I am satisfied is the person in the foregoing instrument named, to whom I first made known the contents thereof, he/she did thereupon acknowledge that he/she signed, sealed and delivered the same as his/her act and deed, for the uses and purposes therein expressed.

____

AFFIX SEAL Notary Public

CHAPTER 3:

EXECUTOR DUTIES: WHAT TO DO IMMEDIATELY AFTER DEATH

Chapter Overview

In this chapter, we'll look at some of the issues that you might need to deal with as executor immediately following the death of the testator.

CHAPTER 3

EXECUTOR DUTIES: WHAT TO DO IMMEDIATELY AFTER DEATH

Introduction

While the death of a loved one can have a huge emotional impact on the surviving family and friends of the deceased person, there nevertheless remains a number of things which need to be tended to during the time commencing immediately after death and before burial. In brief, someone will need to take charge of the whole process of bringing the deceased to his or her final resting place. This process ranges from organizing organ donations, the issue of a death certificate, funeral services and burial arrangements and is often not an easy one. We will take a more detailed look at what's involved over the ensuing pages.

What to Do If Death Occurs at Home

Death at home is quite a common occurrence. In many cases, death at home is planned; in other cases it is completely unexpected and takes immediate family members by complete surprise. Where this happens, in the aftermath of the emotional shock, there are a number of matters which need to be attended to quite promptly. In your capacity as the potential executor of the deceased's estate and/or as a family member or friend, there will be a number of tasks which you can attend to or direct another to tend to in this most difficult of times. Specifically, the following tasks will need to be attended to without undue delay:-

- the deceased's family doctor will need to be contacted and asked to come to the deceased's home in order to pronounce death;

- the nearest relatives of the deceased will need to be contacted, as will anyone else that you believe needs to be informed of the death;
- if the death occurred in unusual circumstances, call the police;
- if the deceased was religious, contact the relevant minister of religion;
- if the deceased wanted to donate any of his organs, speak to the testator's family doctor. Normally where death occurs at home, the general rule is that organs cannot be donated. However, there are some exceptions to this;
- contact an undertaker who will arrange for the laying out of the body and the transporting of the body; and
- find out if the testator has made a will or left any letters of instruction with details of his or her funeral requirements/requests and if so, where it is and who is responsible for dealing with it.

Autopsy Requirements

Autopsies are required by law to determine the cause of death in cases of violent death and death by unknown circumstances. It consists of a simple systematic examination of the body by a pathologist for the purpose of determining the cause of death.

Happily an autopsy is not needed in most natural deaths because enough information can be obtained through the attending physician to determine the cause of death. However, if such information is unavailable, or if circumstances require, an autopsy will be performed. On such occasions an autopsy will be conducted irrespective of the views of the deceased's family, friends and others.

If the deceased had religious beliefs prohibiting an autopsy and you or the family possess a certified letter documenting the deceased's wishes for no autopsy to be performed, this should be supplied to the coroner's office immediately. Most coroners' offices will make every effort possible to honor the deceased's wishes.

Obtain Copies of the Death Certificate

It probably goes without saying, but before even the funeral process can begin, a death certificate must be obtained. This can be obtained from the state offices of vital records or the department of health, but there is some variation from state to state. Alternatively, if it's easier, you can contact the deceased's general practitioner who should be able to procure a copy of same for you.

As previously mentioned, where it is unclear as to how the deceased actually died, it may become necessary for the hospital where the deceased died (or, where the death was at home, the general practitioner who attended to the deceased) to notify the coroner with a view to carrying out an autopsy. In such cases, the death certificate will not be available until after the coroner completes his examination of the deceased.

Once the death certificate has been obtained, the deceased can be formally released in to the care of a funeral director who, in turn, can begin to make funeral arrangements in conjunction with the deceased's family. More importantly for you as executor, however, is that the initial processes for applying for probate can be commenced (although you should at least wait a few days before you commence!!).

For you, as executor, to settle the estate of the deceased you will need to obtain a certified copy (or preferably, for ease, multiple copies) of the death certificate. This is needed to transfer ownership of each piece of real estate, each stock certificate and each motor vehicle and to collect the benefits payable to the deceased's estate under each insurance policy.

Certified copies of the death certificate are also required to access any of the deceased's safe deposit boxes. In addition, financial institutions such as banks and life insurance companies will also generally require a certified copy of the death certificate to allow you access to the accounts and funds of the deceased.

Review Letter of Instruction

Where you have agreed to become an executor for a testator who is still alive, you should encourage them to complete a letter of instruction. A letter of instruction is a document which gives the testator's family and executor or personal representative timely, private and useful information concerning the administration of his/her estate and related matters.

A letter of instruction is guaranteed to ease the burden on the surviving members of the deceased's family by giving them concise and specific information regarding all of the deceased's assets and dealings. It will also greatly reduce the possibility that some of the deceased's assets will remain undiscovered following the deceased's death. The deceased's family member will be extremely grateful for the thoughtfulness and foresight of the deceased in preparing it (as will any executor who has encouraged him to do so).

As letters of instruction are unique to the assets, liabilities and dealing of each author, a one-fits-all template cannot easily be created. However, we will give you some guidance as to what such a letter of instruction/s should contain. However, before we discuss what should be included in the letter, we must first consider who is to receive it and have access to it once the testator writes it. Why? Because that may very well decide what goes into it – especially if there is a degree of sensitivity surrounding the testator's dealings! Of course, there is a simple solution to this problem - two letters could be prepared, one for the family generally and one for the executor's eyes only.

In the example below we have split the letter of instruction into six separate parts namely (i) Emergency Information, (ii) Available Money & Sources of Income & Pensions (iii) Investments & Securities, (iv) Real Estate, (v) Business & Professional Interests and (vi) Miscellaneous. The list below is by no means an exhaustive list, but it's certainly a start!

For ease of description we have used the title "testator" instead of him, her or other to describe the person who would make out the letter for the executor.

(i) Emergency Information

The following emergency information should be included in the testator's letter of instruction:-

- organ donation preferences – in addition to noting the organs to be given, the recipient organization needs to be noted along with a contact telephone number. This is important as the post-mortem medical procedures need to be done promptly;

- where the testator's will is to be found – its exact location;

- autopsy preferences – any significant personal preferences regarding the matter of autopsies should be stated, along with the reasons for such preferences. That way, the testator's views can be taken into consideration by the coroner – subject to state legal requirements!

- funeral and interment preferences – the testator should be encouraged to express his or her wishes, particularly any preferences for religious or secular service and for burial or cremation. It's also a very good idea to attach a list of the names, addresses and phone numbers of people to be notified of the testator's death.

  Also information as to any preferred place of burial or memorial or funeral services already paid for should be included. If the testator is to be cremated they should explain what they want done with their ashes;

- obituary requirements – the preparation of obituaries and eulogies can be very traumatic tasks, so encourage the testator if you can to note down a few points that they would like included and, dependent on the circumstances, you might even encourage the testator to prepare a draft;

- child care – who is to look after the testator's children; and

- animal care – who is to look after the testator's animals.

(ii) Available Money, Sources of Income & Pensions

Details of:-

- checking account/s;

- savings accounts;

- debit and credit cards;

- certificates of deposit;
- employment income – full, part-time or independent;
- alimony;
- child support;
- workers' compensation;
- rental income;
- royalties;
- dividends;
- interest;
- military pension;
- union pension;
- 401(K) plan;
- retirement account; and
- miscellaneous sources of income.

(iii) Investments & Securities

Details of:-

- stocks;
- bonds;
- futures; and
- options.

(iv) Real Estate

Details of:-

- family home;
- holiday home;
- rental property/properties & tenant details;
- timeshare interests; and
- land holdings.

(v) Business & Professional Interests

Details of:-

- sole proprietorships;
- partnership interests;
- shares in companies;
- miscellaneous business interests;
- intellectual property rights; and
- royalties.

(vi) Miscellaneous

Details of:-

- personal information;
- location of personal documents;

- location of personal assets;
- location(s) of safety deposit boxes and envelopes – who has access;
- existence of debts;
- medical information;
- death plans;
- PIN numbers and passwords;
- address book; and
- professional and other advisors.

The task of setting up an instruction letter can initially be a little time consuming, but once done, you have a template that you can simply add to or subtract from when necessary – no need to completely redo the document every time!

Locate the Will and Other Important Papers

Hopefully you, as the nominated executor, will know exactly where the original will is located. Of course if you don't (and you really should have insisted on knowing where the original was kept after agreeing to be executor) you can always check with the county probate court. A large number of testators file their wills at the local court for safekeeping. Another very likely place that the original will could be found is at the office of the lawyer who prepared it on behalf of the deceased.

Resource!

We would also recommend that you search online will storage databases such as www.legalvaults.com which contains details of the locations of and copies of thousands of wills and other personal documents.

If you only have a photocopy of the will and cannot locate the original you will need to check your particular state's laws to find out the appropriate procedure for proving lost wills. Or alternatively, you may be able to present witnesses who can establish that the original of the copy was actually signed by the testator – some states do permit a copy to be admitted to probate in the place of the original if it can't be found.

Did You Know?

Once a will has been admitted to probate it becomes available to the public for inspection. The registry will provide anyone (upon payment of a small fee) with copies of the will but must retain the original.

Organize Anatomic Gifts

It's probably obvious to all that if a testator wished to make an anatomical gift it would be very unwise if he only mentioned it in his will. Often, by the time the will is read and it is noted that an anatomical gift was intended, it's probably too late to do anything about it.

So in looking at and discussing pre-death planning with the testator, you should suggest that such donations should not only be noted in the will, but more importantly should be specified in a gift document (a document which expressly provides for an anatomical gift such as a donor card), listed in a letter of instruction and also mentioned to immediate family members.

Under the Uniform Anatomical Gift Act, currently the law in all states, any gifts of organs or of the entire body properly made in writing by the deceased must be honored by his or her survivors. In honoring the testator's wishes, the survivors should not delay in making the gift as, although the gift may be rendered unusable by disease or accident, the most common reason for rejection of an anatomical gift is delay. A body or organs need to be received by the donee within a few hours of death.

The testator's survivors, having made efforts in good faith to comply with the deceased's wishes and been unable to transport the body or organ in time to the donee, are free to choose any alternative method of body/organ disposal they wish. This would naturally also be the case should the gift be rejected for some reason by the donee.

If you are made aware in discussions with the testator that he or she intends to make an organ or body donation you need to ensure that you either hold or have access to the donor gift card. Also you should stress the importance to the testator that they get their family onside in relation to the donation so that, when the time comes, it is made without delay – thus reducing the possibility of rejection by the donee.

Once the testator passes away it could well be your duty as executor to organize the carrying out of their instructions regarding organ or body donation; especially if you are the caretaker of the donor card!

When it comes to organ donation, speed is of the essence. If the deceased was caring enough to want to make a donation surely it is everyone's duty to do everything in their power to ensure that that happens?

Did You Know?

Donor cards are also called gift cards, gift documents and anatomical gift cards – the precise name varies from state to state.

You should inquire into any state laws that govern either anatomic gifts and/or autopsies, especially those that stipulate who has the final say regarding funeral arrangements, disposal of the body and responsibility for the funeral bill. While these same laws are frequently violated, (often innocently by families who's grief far outweighs reason) they are very seldom enforced in practice. But a general understanding of the main principles of these laws can help you avoid any potential problems.

Arrange Funeral and/or Memorial Service

A situation that continually causes friction and resentment within families is the question of who has the right to decide on the funeral arrangements to be made for the deceased and how their body is to be disposed. Conflicts more often than not arise from generational differences. Take the case, for example, of a young husband who dies and whose wife prefers a simple secular service followed by a cremation. Her preferences are pitched directly against his parents who want an elaborate (and expensive) religious service, an expensive casket, grave burial and a very expensive marker. Who has the last say – the deceased's spouse or parents?

There is a particular order of who is entitled to make this decision legally (please see below) which does vary slightly from state to state. You should however do everything that can be done to avoid things proceeding down the legal route as that is seldom in everyone's best interests!

While the specific order varies from state to state, the order generally goes as follows:

- surviving spouse;
- adult children;
- parent;
- adult sibling;
- guardian; and
- creditors.

As executor it may or may not be your responsibility to organize the funeral. It all depends on your relationship to the deceased. However, when it comes to paying for the funeral, it will be your duty as executor to ensure that payment is made but not your responsibility – i.e. you will be obliged to ensure that the estate makes the payment where possible but you do not have to make the payment from your own personal resources.

It's not uncommon for a funeral director to require a person to personally guarantee the payment of funeral expenses where the funeral director doesn't have personal knowledge of the deceased; or where there is a legitimate concern as to whether there will be enough assets in the deceased's estate to cover the payments. As an executor, you should never agree to become a guarantor unless you are completely sure that the estate will have sufficient resources to meet the payment when the time comes. Otherwise, you could end up being held personally liable for the debt.

While, even as an executor, you may not be involved in making funeral arrangements for the deceased, you should be aware of what arrangements are being made for the funeral (i.e. to keep an eye on the costs and to ensure that the family of the deceased is not being taken advantage of at an emotional time). As an added protection for the distraught family of a deceased person, the probate court can determine in some circumstances that a funeral director has overcharged the family of the deceased and order the bill be either reduced or even negated.

CHAPTER 4:
MAKING SENSE OF THE WILL AND WHAT TO DO IF THERE ISN'T ONE

Chapter Overview

In this chapter, we will look at what constitutes a valid will and how the deceased's property would be distributed amongst his or her heirs-at-law if he or she has failed to make a valid will.

CHAPTER 4

MAKING SENSE OF THE WILL AND WHAT TO DO IF THERE ISN'T ONE!

Important Note!

While it is important for a number of reasons to have a will, not everyone seems to get around to making one.

However, just making a will is not enough. The testator must ensure that the will is valid. Moreover, the testator must ensure that it provides clear instructions to the executors and trustees regarding the management and distribution of the his or her estate.

So, what happens when there is no will? Well, in a manner of speaking, there is no such thing as someone dying without a will. If a person dies without making a will of their own, the state will enforce a substitute will on them (or more to the point on their estate) with pre-defined rules as to the distribution of their estate!

Determining Whether a Will Is Valid

Assuming that you've now located the testator's will, the next step for you is to determine whether or not it's valid.

In general, in order for a will to be valid, it must:

- be made by a person who has reached the age of majority in his or her state (there are certain exceptions to this general rule – see below);
- be made voluntarily and without pressure from any other person. For this reason, it is not advisable for a potential beneficiary to be present when a testator instructs a lawyer to draw up his or her will;
- be made by someone who is of 'sound and disposing mind';
- be in writing;
- be signed by the testator in the presence of two witnesses (or, three witnesses in the state of Vermont);
- be signed by the witnesses, in the presence of the testator, after he or she has signed it. A beneficiary or their spouse should not be a witness to the signing of the will. If a witness is a beneficiary (or the married partner of a beneficiary), the will is still valid but the beneficiary will not be able to inherit any gift left to them under the will;
- include an attestation clause. This clause simply explains how the will has been signed and witnessed; and
- in Louisiana, be notarized.

Age of Majority

The age of majority is a legal description that denotes the threshold age at which a minor becomes legally responsible for their own actions and decisions. At such point, they legally cease being a minor and all responsibility of their parents and guardians is relinquished. The age of majority differs from state to state. In order to create a valid will, the testator must have reached the age of majority in his or her state of residence.

The table below sets out the age of majority for each state.

Age of Majority in U.S.	
Age 18	Alaska, Arizona, California, Colorado, Connecticut, District of Columbia, Florida, Georgia, Hawaii, Idaho, Illinois, Indiana, Iowa, Kansas, Kentucky, Louisiana, Maine, Maryland, Massachusetts, Michigan, Minnesota, Missouri, Montana, New Hampshire, New Mexico, New Jersey, New York, North Carolina, North Dakota, Oklahoma, Oregon, Pennsylvania, Rhode Island, South Carolina, South Dakota, Texas, Vermont, Washington, West Virginia and Wyoming.
Age 19	Alabama, Delaware and Nebraska.
Age 21	Mississippi.
Graduation or Age 18 - (whichever occurs first)	Ohio and Utah.
Graduation or Age 18 – (whichever occurs later)	Arkansas, Tennessee and Virginia.
Graduation or Age 18 – (whichever occurs first) or Age 19 if still at school	Nevada and Wisconsin.

There are some exceptions however to this general rule. Typically, a person under the age of majority who is married, or who has been married, is deemed of sufficient age to execute their will. Emancipated minors may also execute their will. An underage person who joins the military or is on active military service can also make a will, as can a seaman or naval officer at sea.

Lastly, a court can specifically authorize the making of a will by a minor. This might be approved, for example, where a person under 18 years of age inherited a large amount of money, invented some innovative computer software or created the next 'You Tube' with some friends. In each case, if the minor was shown to be of a disposing capability and the move was deemed prudent, the court might well grant approval for the making of a will in the circumstances.

Mental Capacity

The definition of "sound mind" varies from state to state. Typically, the testator must have been of sound and disposing mind and memory when he or she made their will in order for it to be valid. In other words, the testator needed to have understood:

- what a will was;
- that he or she was actually making their will;
- the general extent of their property;
- who their relatives and potential heirs were; and
- the manner in which their will proposed to distribute his or her property (and be satisfied with that!).

If the testator suffered from any kind of mental disorder such as dementia or Alzheimer's disease, or from an addiction to drugs or alcohol; the mental state analyzed is the mental state at the time the testator made his or her will. For example, suppose the testator developed dementia fifty years after making his or her will, the court would look fifty years back to evaluate the testator's mental state at the time the will was made. Similarly, if the testator suffered from drug or alcohol addiction but was not under the influence when he or she signed the will, he or she will be deemed to have been competent when executing the will (assuming that there was not some other underlying medical condition).

Undue Influence

Another form of mental incapacity is undue influence. Undue influence is the exertion by a third party in a position of trust or authority of any kind of control or influence over another person such that a person signs a contract or other instrument which, absent the influence of the third party, he or she would not have ordinarily signed. A contract or instrument may be set aside as not binding on any party who signs it while under undue influence. This claim is often raised by sibling beneficiaries where one sibling is bequeathed more under the terms of a will than the others.

A common undue influence scenario is where a testator uses a beneficiary's attorney to draft a will. Ideally, an ethical attorney should never agree to take on such a project, but in reality, it does happen. Therefore it's always wise in such circumstances for the testator to get independent legal advice when making a will.

Format of a Will

While all states recognize the validity of written wills, certain states will not recognize oral or holographic wills. As such, it's important to ensure that the will is in writing, and complies with the laws of the testator's state of residence.

Signing of a Will

Wills ordinarily need to be signed (save where it's an oral will – which is recognized in some states). Typically, the testator can either sign his or her own will or direct someone to do so on his or her behalf. Signatures may include marks, initials, a rubber stamp, a 'nick-name', or a former name.

Witnessing a Will

While each state has its own laws setting out how the execution of a will should be witnessed these tend to be quite similar from state to state. Generally speaking, in order for a will to be valid, the testator needs to have signed his or her name to the will in the presence of two or, in the case of Vermont, three witnesses. In turn, the witnesses should sign their names in the presence of the testator and in the presence of each other.

Notarizing a Will

Only in the state of Louisiana must a will be notarized. In all other states notarization is not required — however it is recommended. With notarization, each of the witnesses sign a document called a 'self-proving affidavit'. This is an affidavit sworn by the witnesses which eliminates the need for them to later testify that they witnessed the testator signing the will. This affidavit must be sworn before a notary public.

Reading of the Will

As an executor, you should read the will as soon as possible following the death of the testator. Where possible, you should only read the original signed version of the will rather than a copy. Copies run the risk of being incomplete, inaccurate and, in some cases, invalid due to revocation (this is where the will has been cancelled by the creation of a later will or destruction of the original).

Although more and more wills these days are written in clear modern language a good number are still written in an old fashioned legalistic style. As such, it's important to take your time and read the will thoroughly. You may not understand all the legal jargon the first time round, so don't be hesitant about re-reading the will until you are satisfied that you fully understand it. If there are any terms that you do not understand, look them up in your local library or from a valid and reliable source on the internet. If you are still in doubt, pick up the phone and speak to an attorney. It's important that you understand the provisions of the will as this will make things a lot easier for you when it comes to distributing the estate.

Also, in general, the reading of a will can provide you with a good deal of information regarding the testator and his or her estate, including details of his or her children, heirs, assets, liabilities, funeral requirements, anatomic gift preferences and so on.

Notifying Beneficiaries and Others

Once you determine that a will is valid, you should notify the parties who will have an interest in the testator's estate under the terms of the will. Where a beneficiary under the will is a minor, you will need to notify the child's parents or guardian. Often wills identify who this is. If a beneficiary is mentally incompetent, you should notify their custodian or conservator. Typically, the parties who need to be notified include:

- beneficiaries and alternate beneficiaries under the will;
- heirs-at-law – even where they do not appear to be entitled under the will; and
- the spouse and the children, if any, of the deceased.

Important Task

Duty to inform heirs and beneficiaries under the probate code.

Not later than 30 days after his or her appointment every executor must give information of his or her appointment to the heirs and beneficiaries under a will. The information should be delivered or sent by ordinary mail to each of the heirs and beneficiaries. The information shall include the name and address of the personal representative, indicate that it is being sent to persons who have or may have some interest in the estate being administered, indicate whether a bond has been filed, and detail the Court where papers relating to the estate are on file. The information shall state that the estate is being administered by the personal representative under the [State] Probate Code without supervision by the Court but that recipients are entitled to information regarding the administration from the personal representative and can petition the Court in any matter relating to the estate, including distribution of assets and expenses of administration.

The executor's failure to give this information is a breach of duty but does not affect the validity of his or her appointment, powers or other duties.

Dying Intestate

When a person dies without a valid will or if a will cannot be located, is deemed false, or invalid for not meeting statutory elements; the person is said to have died intestate. However, even where a person has not actually made out their own will, they will still be deemed, in a manner of speaking, to have a will – it's just that the will is a state imposed 'substitute will' derived from the rules of intestate succession! The terms of this will depend on the intestacy laws of the state in which the deceased was resident at the time he or she died.

Did You Know?

Over 2.4 million Americans die every year (Source: National Vital Statistics Report). Of this number, research by FindLaw indicates that almost 55% haven't made a will and, of those that have made a will (being the other 45%), 12% of those people end up with invalid wills. Therefore a total of approximately 67% of Americans die annually without a valid will.

This 'substitute will', or rules of intestacy as they are properly called, specifies how the estate will be administered and just who is entitled to receive a gift or inheritance from that estate. In some cases of course the 'state imposed will' reflects exactly what the deceased would have wanted anyway, but in most cases it does not.

State laws cover such things as the following items:

- the making up of a list of persons entitled to be appointed as administrator – a person who will have similar duties and responsibilities to an executor of the estate;
- a listing of people entitled to by appointed as guardian for the deceased's minor children;
- the powers that will be granted to the administrator and the rules under

which he/she must be bonded; and

- the identity of persons entitled to inherit the deceased's estate – referred to as "heirs-at-law".

Where a person dies intestate, the intestacy laws of the state of residence of the deceased person will determine who gets what from their estate. Generally, the rule of thumb here is that the first in line to benefit is the surviving spouse and then the children of the deceased. However, if there is no surviving spouse or children, then the general rule of thumb is 'the bigger the estate, the more — and more distant — the relatives who get to share.'

The Main Differences Between Dying "Testate" and "Intestate"?

Testate	Intestate
There is a valid will.	There is no will, or the will is invalid.
The will has been signed by the testator.	There is no will, or the will is invalid.
The estate of the deceased is referred to as a "testate" estate.	The estate of the deceased is referred to as an "intestate" estate.
The person dealing with the winding up of the estate will be known as the "executor of the will" or as the "personal representative".	The person dealing with the winding up of the estate will be known as the "administrator of the estate".
The personal representative will need to file a petition for probate of a will & letters testamentary.	The administrator will need to file a petition for letters of administration.
The person named in the will acts as executor or personal representative.	The administrator will be appointed in accordance with the rule of priority set out under state law.

The Main Differences Between Dying "Testate" and "Intestate"?	
The people who receive gifts under a will are called "beneficiaries".	The people who receive distributions on intestacy are called "heirs" or "heirs-at-law".
The beneficiaries are named in the will.	The heirs are determined in accordance with the rules of priority set out under state law.

Partial Intestacy

In addition to providing for situations where a person has died without making a will, intestacy laws also apply to situations where the testator has failed to deal with all of their property under the terms of their will. This is called a partial intestacy.

Partial intestacy commonly occurs where a will fails to include what's known as a residuary clause. A residuary clause simply provides that any of the deceased's property which has not been specifically gifted under the terms of the will is to be given to a named beneficiary or beneficiaries known as the residuary beneficiary/beneficiaries. A partial intestacy can also occur where the residuary beneficiary or beneficiaries die before the testator and no alternate beneficiaries are named to receive the residue of the estate in their place.

Did You Know?

A partial intestacy occurs where a testator fails to dispose of their entire estate under their will. In such cases, property not specifically disposed of under their will generally becomes the subject of intestate administration proceedings.

Appointment of an Administrator

The term administrator is the name given to the person appointed to administer an intestate estate (an estate where no will exists, or where none can be found). The deceased's close relatives usually have the highest priority for appointment by the court as administrator. It follows that if the person at the top of the priority list declines then the next person down the list is asked to do the job.

But, if no member of the family is willing to serve, a creditor may apply to the court (naturally because he or she wishes the estate to pay his claim quickly) for appointment as administrator. Any such petition is only granted after all the heirs have been duly notified.

While the entitlement of persons to be appointed as administrators of a deceased person's estate varies from state to state, it generally goes in the following order:

- surviving spouse or domestic partner;
- children;
- grandchildren;
- other descendents;
- parents;
- brothers and sisters;
- descendents of brothers and sisters;
- grandparents;
- descendents of grandparents;
- children of a predeceased spouse or domestic partner;
- other descendents of a predeceased spouse or domestic partner;
- other next of kin;

- parents of a predeceased spouse or domestic partner;
- descendents of parents of a predeceased spouse or domestic partner;
- conservator or guardian of the estate acting in that capacity at the time of death who has filed a first account and is not acting as conservator or guardian for any other person;
- public administrator;
- creditors; or
- any other suitable person.

If there is an intestacy or a partial intestacy, be sure to check the state intestacy laws of the deceased's state of residence to determine who exactly can be lawfully appointed as administrator. Also, certain states impose time limits on how long the rules of priority apply. Once these time limits expire, which in some cases can occur in 40 days or less following the descendents passing, any 'suitable person' can apply to the court to be appointed as administrator of the deceased's estate. Check your state requirements in this respect.

Distribution of Assets on Intestacy

While intestacy laws generally vary from state to state, this variance has been greatly lessened by the Uniform Probate Code (the "Code") which, at the time of this writing, has been adopted by 18 states in full and by numerous states in part. The Code is a good place to begin a general discussion on this topic. However, you must check your own state law for a more sophisticated and thorough understanding of the Code. The law that usually applies is the state law of your domicile, or principal place residence.

UNIFORM PROBATE CODE - FULL STATE ADOPTIONS		
Alaska	Michigan	North Dakota
Arizona	Minnesota	Pennsylvania
Colorado	Montana	South Carolina
Hawaii	Nebraska	South Dakota
Idaho	New Jersey	Utah
Maine	New Mexico	Wisconsin

The Code, provides that priority of inheritance is given to the following persons in the following order:

- surviving spouse;
- descendents (children, grandchildren, etc.);
- parents;
- descendents of deceased's parents (siblings, nieces and nephews);
- grandparents; and
- descendents of grandparents (aunts and uncles and cousins).

Under the Code, relatives are each apportioned a certain percentage of the deceased's estate. The percentages are as follows:

Share of Surviving Spouse

The share of a surviving spouse is calculated as follows:-

- A surviving spouse is entitled to the entire estate if neither the deceased's descendants (i.e. children, grandchildren and great grandchildren) nor the deceased's parents have survived the deceased.
- If the deceased's parents survive but no descendents survive the deceased, the surviving spouse is entitled to the first $200,000 of the estate plus ¾ of anything exceeding that amount.

- If the deceased is survived by a spouse and descendants from that marriage only, the surviving spouse will take the first $150,000 of the estate plus ½ of anything exceeding that amount, plus all community property.

- If the deceased is survived by descendents from the marriage to the surviving spouse and by descendents from someone other than his or her surviving spouse, the surviving spouse takes the first $100,000 of the estate plus ½ of anything exceeding that amount, plus all community property.

Share of Descendents

- If the deceased's spouse does not survive the deceased and the deceased's descendants do, then the deceased's descendents take the entire estate.

- In some cases, if the deceased's child has predeceased the deceased, that child's surviving children will inherit their parent's share of the intestate estate. This is known as 'per stirpes' distribution.

Share of Parents

- If the deceased is not survived by a spouse or descendents, his or her entire net estate passes to his or her parents equally or, if only one survives, to the survivor.

Share of Other Relatives

- If neither the deceased's spouse, descendents, nor parents survive the deceased, the entire net estate passes to the deceased's siblings. If there are no siblings or no descendents of the deceased's siblings, the deceased's estate goes to any surviving grandparents or their descendents.

Even with all these intestacy provisions, if the deceased dies without a will and without traceable relatives or relatives that fall within the scope of the Code or state intestacy provisions, the ultimate successor will be the state treasury!

Important Note

The administrator of the intestate estate is required to exercise great diligence in identifying and locating the 'heirs-at-law'.

Resource

For more specific information and an intestacy estate calculator please visit www.mystatewill.com/specific_states.htm.

CHAPTER 5:
EXECUTOR DUTIES: TAKING STOCK

Chapter Overview

In this chapter, we look at some of the steps that you should take during the first few weeks following the death of the deceased. In particular, we look at how you can provide for the immediate needs of the family and also at some of the preliminary steps which you could take to protect the value of the deceased's estate.

CHAPTER 5

EXECUTOR DUTIES: TAKING STOCK

Estimate Cash Needed for Immediate Future

Generally speaking, more often than not the most immediate concern for dependents when a loved one passes away is the availability of funds to cover the funeral expenses and to discharge ordinary day-to-day living expenses such as mortgage repayments, educational fees, utility bills, grocery bills and so on.

Given the trauma which the family of the deceased is most likely going through immediately following the deceased's death, they are often too emotionally distraught to deal with financial matters. As an executor, you can provide invaluable assistance to the deceased's family at that particular point in time by organizing funds to meet their urgent and ongoing needs.

Remember, during the probate process, the majority of the deceased's assets will be frozen until the Grant of Probate or Letters issue (this is the document that legally allows the executor to deal with the assets of the deceased). As such, you will need to consider how best to procure funds to meet the family's immediate needs. You can usually do this in one of two ways.

Firstly, many financial institutions offer loans to heirs and beneficiaries who are waiting to receive inheritances. In many cases, assuming that the beneficiary meets the financial requirements of the bank in question, money can be advanced in as little as 72 hours. However, it's important to read the small print. Unlike a standard loan, many of these financial institutions take an assignment of the beneficiary's right to receive an element or amount of their inheritance. As there are often no loan repayments or no interest repayments on this loan, the amount assigned includes a premium for putting the facility in place. This premium can be exceptionally high in cases so beware. All that said, it should be possible to secure a fairly standard loan with standard repayment obligations from a regular bank if needed.

The second and better way for the family of the deceased to get their hands on funds derives from the fact that not all assets need to go through probate; and as such are not frozen pending completion of the probate process. These assets include items such as insurance proceeds, assets held in a living trust, joint bank accounts, property held in joint tenancy or assets passing to a designated beneficiary on death. While we talk about assets that don't go through probate in much more detail in Chapter 7, suffice to say for the moment that these assets can provide an immediate life line to the family and can often be accessed with just the death certificate of the deceased. However, be careful as extracting the proceeds payable under a life policy, for example, may take a number of weeks or even months notwithstanding that there may be a beneficiary designated under the policy itself.

With the family's consent and the consent of all beneficiaries under the will, you could also consider selling some of the deceased's personal property (which is not normally frozen by probate) in order to raise money. For example, you could sell furniture, cars, collectibles, etc.

The state also does its bit in providing for the needs of a surviving spouse and minor children by providing 'financial assistance' for the surviving spouse as well as the deceased's minor children. This financial assistance comes in the form of "homestead rights". This is a right given to the deceased's family to remain in and occupy the deceased's home for a period of time — even in the case where the home has been left to someone else! However, while the state does its bit, it's too often insufficient to provide for the needs of the deceased's family throughout the entire probate process! As such, you should consider all options available to the family in order to facilitate them through the entire probate process – which can go on for over a year in some cases!

Unfortunately, however, there are often occasions when no funds are immediately available. What do you do if the banks are unwilling to make arrangements to help the survivors out? Well, you may have to use your position as executor to arrange a loan for the survivor until the assets of the estate are released and distributed. In most cases, executors will be able to take out a loan out in the name of the surviving spouse and secure it against the property of the deceased held in probate (which may even include real estate!). You will need to speak to the bank in relation to any such loan; and preferably a bank with whom the deceased and/or his or her family had/have a good relationship as this should make matters easier to facilitate.

Reducing Expenses During those First Few Days

One of the too often overlooked, yet important, tasks that you should attend to in the first few days following a death is the reduction of on-going expenses. This task becomes much more important where the family of the deceased have limited funds available to them until probate of the deceased's estate completes.

It's important to reduce expenses immediately because in death, while revenues generally cease immediately (salary or social security for example), expenses continue to accrue indefinitely. In practice, you will need to sort through, with the assistance of the deceased's family, the personal papers of the deceased in order to see what ongoing outgoings he or she may still have in place.

Here are just a few suggestions as to what come be done: cancel absolutely everything that isn't really required anymore – the deceased's health insurance, phone service, utilities, certain insurances (for example phone insurance, credit card insurance, travel insurance etc), newspaper and magazine subscriptions, club memberships, sports memberships – this list is by no means exhaustive, everyone has something they can add. This cancellation exercise has a dual benefit – the expense stops immediately and within a few weeks you may well be getting refunds running into thousands of dollars!

Determine Various Special Needs (e.g. Minor Children)

If the deceased left children but no surviving spouse, you will need to consider whether a guardian and/or conservator will need to be appointed if none has been appointed under the terms of the deceased's will. The appointment itself will usually involve a court application and, as such, you should speak to an attorney in order to determine what exactly needs to be done in order to progress the application.

However, in the interim, you will need to consider which of the testator's relatives (or those of a deceased spouse or partner) or friends would be best suited to care for the deceased's children. This is by no means a simple decision and you should afford due thought and consideration before reaching a conclusion. If appropriate and depending on their age, you may wish to discuss the matter directly with the children in question. Also, review the will to determine if the deceased had appointed any guardians.

Important Note

Whenever possible, we strongly recommend that an executor discusses all possible guardianship scenarios with the testator before the will is made or as soon as the executor becomes aware of his or her appointment (assuming of course that this happens before the testator passes away) so that proper provision can be made for the testator's children and so that the executor is aware of all of the options.

Initial Inspection and Protection of Property

While you will not actually be officially appointed as executor until the formal probate process commences, you should (assuming you have not decided to refuse to accept the role) still consider taking steps to locate and secure the deceased's assets - be it by insurance cover or otherwise.

There are a number of steps that you can take to locate as many assets as possible. For instance, you can inspect the deceased's bank records and files as well as open any safe deposit boxes held by the deceased. We will discuss the mechanics of this latter point in much more detail below, so for now please just bear it in mind as a preliminary task that you need to tend to.

As an executor, you will also be responsible for the inspection and securing of any real estate in the estate including the continuance or termination of any relevant utilities, as well as, the examination and updating (if necessary) of any fire, casualty and other business insurance. In certain instances, depending on the circumstances, it may even be necessary to consider organizing security systems or personnel to protect the property.

Important Note

As an executor you will be responsible for the protection of all of the assets of the estate. This includes protection from theft, fire, loss and destruction. If you fail to preserve the assets, you could be held personally liable. A simple, way to protect the estate's assets is to take them into your personal possession. This should especially be done in the case of valuable documents. By taking them in to your possession, we are not simply suggesting that you bring them home and place them in a drawer! They should be placed in a secured storage facility and, where appropriate, should be insured for full value.

Another important duty of an executor is the assessment of any ongoing small business (previously operated either by the testator either alone, in partnership with others or through a corporation or company). You may very well be required to make preliminary management decisions about the running needs of any such business even though the business may operate outside your area of expertise. In such cases, you should consider engaging the services of a professional director, an accountant or other professional who can properly assist with and advise on running the business. In any event, when confronted with the possibility of running a business, it's best to discuss the matter with the deceased's former business partners, any family members or friends that may have been involved in the business with the deceased and/or professional advisors.

Important Note

We would again recommend that, where possible, an executor should have a full and detailed discussion with the testator as to how his or her business would be managed in the short term following his/her death. This may save the business thousands of dollars and prevent a depletion in the ultimate value of the testator's estate.

CHAPTER 6:

WHAT AN EXECUTOR SHOULD DO IN THE FIRST MONTH

Chapter Overview

In this chapter, we will look at the tasks than an executor must deal with during the first month following his or her appointment. These tasks include establishing appropriate filing systems, reducing outgoings of the estate and managing the assets of the estate. By the end of this chapter, your obligations as executor will become a lot clearer to you!

CHAPTER 6

WHAT AN EXECUTOR SHOULD DO IN THE FIRST MONTH

Introduction

During the first month following the death of the deceased, you will need to prepare yourself for the task ahead. This preparation ranges from getting yourself physically organized for the tasks ahead, understanding the probate process and locating, collecting and managing the estate assets pending their distribution to the beneficiaries named under the deceased's will. We will explore each of these aspects in more detail below.

PART 1 - GETTING ORGANIZED

Set Up a Filing System to Cover Probate & Estate Matters

Being well organized and maintaining an appropriate filing system is critical to ensuring your success as an executor. You will need to set up a filing system that allows you to keep track of paper work relating to the deceased's estate – as well as any notes that you have made along the way. This will help you when it comes to dealing with claims against the estate and dealing with financial institutions and beneficiaries.

Important Note

Be careful not to lose any papers relating to the probate of the deceased's estate or to mix these papers up with your own. This could lead to a situation where you forget about certain assets and close probate of the estate without ever transferring the assets to the rightful beneficiary. If this happens, you may need to re-open probate!

With a little thought, setting up a simple filing system should be a relatively straightforward task. Typically, there are two particular filing systems that you could use. You could either establish a system based on subject category (for example, income, expenses, assets, liabilities) or, alternatively, some form of numerical system. The choice is yours. You can use whatever system makes the most sense to you.

Organizing By Category

The first step in the process will be to sort through your papers and discard anything that you don't need. Alternatively, if you don't wish to discard certain papers, it may be useful to place them in a miscellaneous file.

The next step is to sort the papers into various piles or categories. You could consider using some of the following categories:-

- bank statements;
- birth certificates and other personal records;
- brokerage account statements;
- business agreements;
- child support documents;
- credit card statements;

- disability-related documents;
- divorce papers;
- employment related matters;
- insurance policies, statements, or bills;
- investment records;
- pension records;
- post office;
- prenuptial agreement;
- real estate deeds and tax records;
- registration papers for vehicles or boats;
- retirement account statements;
- service providers (e.g., landscapers, trash haulers, etc.);
- social security records;
- state health/welfare departments;
- utility companies; and
- miscellaneous.

Once you have decided on your categories, create a file or sub file for each category. Clearly label each category. Then sort through the papers that you wish to keep and place them into appropriate categories. If none of the categories seem appropriate, don't be afraid to create a new category – but, remember, don't complicate matters too much.

We recommend placing your files in a suitable filing cabinet or filing system so that the records can be easily accessed and maintained in the future.

Organizing By Number

Similar to the categories system, decide on the papers that you want to keep. Now sort them into bundles. For each bundle, you will create a numerical file. You will then create an index or a spreadsheet identifying that file by reference to its number and detailing the contents of that file. Each new file is given a new number and an appropriate description. When you need to find something, you can simply do a word search of your spreadsheet. If you have properly identified the contents of the file, your search should reveal the number of the file in which the required information is stored.

Of course, the big disadvantage of organizing by numbers or index filing is that you must keep the spreadsheet or document log updated. This can be tedious work, especially if there is a large amount of paperwork associated with the estate.

Filing Tips

Many people often find it easier to organise files by number or alphabetically so that they can be easily found when required. People also like to use similar coloured files or similar coloured tabs for related sub-categories. This helps to find the file a lot quicker – especially if the files are placed in a well packed cabinet.

Obtain a Tax Identification Number

Before you can deal with the deceased's estate, you will need to obtain an employer's tax identification number or taxpayer identification numbers as they are also called. These identification numbers will need to be provided when dealing with financial institutions and other third parties.

The process of obtaining a new employer identification number is quite straight forward. All you need to do is complete an Internal Revenue Service Form SS-4 and return it to the IRS. Once processed, the IRS should issue you with a tax identification number for the estate. You can obtain the relevant form from the IRS website at http://www.irs.gov/formspubs/index.html.

Important Note

All transactions carried out by the estate should be done in the estate's name and using the estate's tax identification number.

Open a Bank Account in the Name of the Estate

The opening of a bank account in the name of the estate goes hand in hand with your obligation to maintain proper financial records for the estate. By using a designated bank account, you will be able to use the account statement to help keep track of all payments made and all benefits received by the estate.

As an executor, you will have the choice of which financial institution you wish to open the account with. In practice, many executors tend to open an account with either the bank with whom they personally deal for their own day to day affairs or with the deceased's bank. Of course, you are more than entitled to evaluate and use other banks especially if it makes financial or commercial sense to do so in the circumstances.

Financial institutions provide varying services that may be required by an executor of an estate. These include services such as the provision of loans, share valuations, trust services, investment management and so on. In deciding on which institution to use, it's important that you properly evaluate the services provided by the institution in question, the likelihood that you will requires these services and the likely fees associated with engaging the banks to act in these matters. If chosen correctly, the right financial institution can help you keep legal and other fees down.

Pay attention to the interest rates offered by the various financial institutions – remember the estate's monies may be sitting in the account for a number of months or even years. Where there is a large amount of money sitting in the account, interest payments can be quite significant.

Important Note

Safety checks

When making payments from the estate, it's useful to use 'safety checks'. These are similar to standard checks and can be purchased from most banks. The big difference is that every time you write a check, the details are input on to a carbon copy at the back of the check. You use this carbon copy to help maintain your records of estate transactions.

Once you have an account set up, you should transfer all the estate's cash and monies to this account and, after that, ensure that all of the estate's transactions are put through that account. It's also important that you only use one account so as to avoid the risk of accidentally mixing up the funds with other monies! Believe it or not this happens quite frequently especially where an executor is the surviving spouse of the deceased. Beware - it's very easy to mix up funds which pass outside probate (such as certain insurance payments or payments under a pay-on-death account) and claims for other benefits owing directly to the estate. You should take appropriate measures to avoid this happening.

PART II

SEARCHING FOR AND LOCATING ESTATE ASSETS

Sort Through the Deceased's Personal Belongings

As an executor, you will need to carry out a thorough search for all of the deceased's assets and liabilities. It will be your sole responsibility to locate these assets, pay any taxes owing on them and, finally, to distribute the assets to the beneficiaries named in the deceased's will. Typically, these assets will include items such as real estate, cash, investments, vehicles, social security payments, bank accounts, furniture, antiques, artwork, jewelry, pension plans, IRAs, stocks, brokerage accounts, shares in privately held companies and businesses, partnership interests, life insurance and so on.

Finding assets and determining liabilities is not always an easy task. In some cases the deceased's assets or liabilities may be readily identifiable from the deceased's own personal files or, in the case of assets, may be conveniently located in the deceased's home. However, in the majority of cases, you will need to carefully review the deceased's personal records and correspondence to establish the assets held or liabilities owing by the deceased at the time of his death.

In carrying out your search, there are a number places where you can start. We recommend that you review the following:-

- any letter of instruction left by the deceased;
- the deceased's check books and banks accounts;
- the deceased's mail; and
- any safe deposit box held by the deceased.

Review Letter of Instruction

The task of discovering assets and liabilities will of course be a lot easier if the deceased left an up-to-date letter of instruction (please see Chapter 3 for a full explanation) listing all of the deceased's current assets and liabilities, a description of each plus its exact location. You should of course allow for any assets or liabilities that may have been overlooked and therefore not included in this list. To cover this shortfall, you will still need to review the deceased's other personal records.

Of course, if there is no letter of instruction and you are not really aware of, or familiar with, the deceased's financial dealings you will just have to carry out your search the hard way!

Review Check Books and Bank Accounts

One of the best and most fruitful places to start your review is with the deceased's financial records. A review of the deceased's check book, cancelled checks, bank statements and credit card statements can reveal a huge amount about the deceased's incomes and expenses. Usually, it's both prudent and useful to review each record or statement on a transaction by transaction basis for the three years prior to the deceased's death.

The records will give you great clues to both assets and liabilities. For instance you will find direct debit details, or check stubs of checks that have been written, for such items as:

- annual subscriptions – magazines, charities, etc;
- charge card accounts;
- dividends;
- insurance policies – travel, medical, vehicle, house, business, etc;
- license fees for cars, boats, guns, business, etc;
- loans – personal, business, etc;
- memberships – gyms, clubs, professional, etc;

- monthly savings, investments, etc;
- mortgage payments;
- payments to brokers;
- rental receipts;
- royalties;
- social security receipts;
- taxes – personal, business, etc;
- rental payments – property, cars, machinery, equipment, etc;
- utility payments – gas, electricity, telephone, cell phone, etc; and
- so on…..

The items listed above are just a sampling of the many items you will come across.

Important Task

Upon discovery, cancel all non-essential ongoing expenditures and seek refunds where appropriate.

In addition to reviewing the records and statements, you should also contact each financial institution at which the deceased held an account to determine the various accounts held by the deceased there and also the balance of those accounts at the date of death. In most cases, the financial institution will ask for a copy of the letters of authority as well as a certified copy of the death certificate of the deceased. Certain institutions may require additional documentation but they will generally advise you where such documents are required.

In certain states, banks and other financial institutions will require the approval of the state taxing authority before it will release the proceeds of an account to the executor of an estate. This approval is not very difficult to obtain, particularly where the beneficiaries of the deceased's estate are close family members of the deceased.

The Deceased's Mail

One of the best sources of information regarding the deceased's affairs will come from the deceased's mail. In addition to personal correspondence, the mail will often contain helpful items such as professional correspondence, bank statements, portfolio statements, dividend checks and so on. These documents will all provide useful information regarding the deceased's assets and liabilities.

In order to get the mail, you can of course call around to the deceased's home or former place of business and collect it. However, it often makes more sense to re-direct the deceased's post to your home address or office. In order to re-direct the post, you will need to contact the U.S. Postal Service directly. In the absence of contacting them, they will continue to deliver the mail to the deceased's residence. A member of the deceased's family can usually change the postal address with a copy of the death certificate and personal identification. However, as an executor you will need to produce evidence of your appointment as executor of the deceased's estate. Usually, the post office will look for a copy of your letters of authority. As you may not yet have your letters of authority (we'll discuss obtaining your letters of authority in more detail in Chapter 8) you should consult with the deceased's family to make arrangements. You should contact your local post office in order to get a copy of the form that you will need to complete to register the change of address.

While dealing with the deceased's mail, you might also consider taking the opportunity to have the deceased's name removed from commercial marketing lists. The Direct Marketing Association (DMA) maintains a Deceased Do Not Contact list. All DMA members are obliged to remove any names appearing on this list from their own mailing lists. Indeed, many non-DMA members review this list and remove the names from their own mailing lists. Once a name is registered with the DMA, both solicited and non-solicited commercial mail should begin to decrease within a few months. To register a name or learn more, you can visit the DMA website at *www.the-dma.org*.

Safe Deposit Box

If the deceased's records reveal the existence of a safe deposit box, you will want to open it as soon as possible in order to check the contents. Often, safe deposit boxes contain important legal documents such as title deeds, stock certificates, bearer bonds, wills, powers of attorney and so on. In addition, they can often contain jewelry, cash and important physical possessions.

However, before rushing off to open a safe deposit box, it's important that you first understand some of the legalities around how they are 'held' and how they can be opened.

A safe deposit box can be held or registered in the name of one or more people. Where it is held by one person, the holder may designate someone with authority to access it. Where it is held by two people as joint holders, a surviving joint owner will have access to the box after the other joint holder dies. However, if the deceased was the sole registered owner of the box, the bank will typically deny access to the box until an executor or personal representative of the deceased's estate is appointed.

Did You Know?

There are significant legal consequences associated with the joint holding of a safe deposit box or indeed any other assets. Legal advice may therefore be required when dealing with this.

However, on certain occasions, the bank will open the safe deposit box under bank supervision for the purpose of determining whether it contains the deceased's will.

Historically, safe deposit boxes were sealed upon the death of the registered owner in order to secure the payment of state inheritance tax. The boxes could only be opened in the presence of a tax official who would carry out an inventory of its contents. Since state inheritance taxes have been abolished in the majority of states, this limitation should not be a concern in most cases. However, you should check with the bank maintaining the safe deposit box or with an attorney registered in that state as to whether any legalities apply. If there are any formalities, the bank or attorney will advise you on how to proceed.

Whether or not any formalities apply to the opening of a safe deposit box, it's good practice to have a witness attend with you when you are opening a safe deposit box. It's often useful to prepare an inventory in the presence of the witness and have them sign their name at the bottom of the inventory to confirm its accuracy.

PART III

CLAIMING BENEFITS

Claim Any Unpaid Salary, Insurance and Any Other Benefits

If the surviving spouse or children of the deceased have not already done so, you should organize for the collection of any salary, wages, accumulated vacation and/or sick pay and other fringe benefits that may be owing to the deceased.

It should be noted that the laws of some states permit the direct payment to the surviving spouse, adult children or other next of kin, of salary and other benefits without proceeding through probate. You, as executor, or the deceased's family members should have little trouble in collecting this from the deceased's employer, although some smaller companies may not be as familiar with the law on this point. In the event of difficulty obtaining payment or undue delay in doing so you should consider engaging an attorney to assist you and, if necessary, file a complaint with the state Department of Labor through a small claims court.

There are numerous different types of benefits that can be claimed including, amongst others:

- life Insurance and annuities;
- mortgage insurance;
- widow's social security benefits;
- employment retirement plan benefits;
- bank account benefits that are payable on death;
- savings bond benefits;

- veteran's benefits;
- social security benefits;
- redeeming traveler's checks; and
- redeeming unused airplane tickets and prepaid travel.

In addition to the above, if there are circumstances which would lead you to the conclusion that the deceased's death occurred as a result of the willful act or negligence of a third party, you should consult an attorney as the estate may be entitled to take a wrongful death action against any person or organization responsible for the deceased's death. The majority of cases for wrongful death are based on claims for medical misdiagnosis, medical negligence, dangerous driving or on negligence of some other description.

PART IV

MANAGING THE ESTATE

Managing the Estate

As an executor, it will be your responsibility to ensure that the estate pays any bills that the deceased had outstanding (such as utility or credit card invoices) at the time of his or her death. You can discharge these debts from the existing funds within the estate, from benefits paid to the estate following the deceased's death and from debts owing to the estate at the time of the deceased's death and subsequently recovered.

The management of the estate can be quite straightforward at times. In most cases, executors simply need to manage the estate bank account, pay debts, acknowledge and assess claims against the estate and so on. However, on occasion, matters can become more compacted. For example, if the deceased owned a business, you may have to buy or sell certain assets to ensure the survival of the business, make payroll distributions, temporarily run the business (or at the very least, find someone to do it) until it is passed on to the deceased's heirs (of course, the deceased could stipulate in his or her will that the business be sold or give the executor authority to sell it in order to distribute the estate!).

Similar issues could arise where the deceased had large real estate portfolios or complex investment structures. In which case you will most likely need to consult a professional advisor in order to understand how these interests can be passed on to the estate's beneficiaries in a tax efficient manner. Remember, the cost of engaging a professional advisor will be a cost of the estate and not a personal cost of yours – so do not hesitate to engage a professional where you feel it appropriate or necessary.

So, when you are faced with managing the estate, where do you start? What do you do first? Well, one of the first things that you need to do is to prevent the depletion of value from the estate. This is done in two ways – firstly, by cutting off any unnecessary expenditures being incurred by the estate and secondly, by liquidating any assets which are depreciating in value. After that, it's important that the remaining assets are secured and managed until such time as they are ready to be distributed to the beneficiaries under the will. Remember, as an executor, it is your responsibility to ensure that the value of the estate is preserved until that time.

Send Death Notices to the Utilities, Banks and Credit Card Companies

As soon as possible after the death of the deceased, you should commence the process of cancelling all non-essential payments being made by the estate.

In order to do this, you will need to send notifications of cancellation to each relevant party together with a copy of the deceased's death certificate and your letters of authority (if issued).

You will need to contact the various utility companies in order to cancel all non-essential utilities such as gas, electricity, water, telephone etc. However, you need to be careful in selecting which utilities you wish to terminate. Perhaps the deceased's family will remain in the deceased's house? Maybe the house will be vacant but a harsh winter is expected so it would be prudent to leave the heat on to prevent dampness? Maybe the electricity needs to be kept on in order to operate the security system? Maybe the deceased sub-let his premises to a third party and they need access to the utilities?

The decision to terminate a utility is therefore one which should only be made after due consideration of all related matters.

However, apart from the utilities, there is noting to prevent you from notifying the banks and credit card companies and requesting that they cease all payments immediately – including both direct debits and standing orders. However, similar to the position above regarding utilities, the payments should only be stopped after a careful review as to why they are being made.

As mentioned above, in the case of bank accounts, it's useful to have the funds contained in the deceased's accounts transferred to the estate bank account so that you can easily keep track of payments from one central location.

You will also need to notify the deceased's creditors of the deceased's death so that they can present any claims that they might have against the estate. The payment of creditors is a complicated area. As such, we'll cover the topic in much more detail in Chapter 9.

The deceased's mail is a good place to start to determine who or what institutions should be notified. However, typically, the following tend to be notified quite regularly:-

- banks;
- credit card companies;
- utility companies;
- post office;
- doctors or other health care providers;
- employer and former employers;
- investment firms;
- insurance companies;
- landlord or tenants;
- pension payers;
- service providers (e.g., landscapers, trash haulers, etc.);
- social security administration;
- state health/welfare departments; and
- veteran affairs department.

Remember that, in certain instances, where you notify the Social Security Administration (www.ssa.gov) of the deceased's death, they may require you to return or refund any check received by the deceased in the month in which he or she died.

Finally, if the deceased was in receipt of spousal or child support from a spouse or former spouse, you should advise the spouse or former spouse of the deceased's death.

Cancel Unnecessary Estate Outgoings

As mentioned above, it's important to cancel all unnecessary outgoings of the estate. In this respect, you should:-

- terminate any rental arrangements which the deceased had whereby he/she rented or leased property as a tenant/lessee (be it for personal or commercial purposes) at the time of his/her death. Remember, in addition to real estate, such arrangement may include hire purchase equipment arrangements, vehicle leasing arrangements and much more. Alternatively, if it is not possible to terminate the arrangement, consider sub-letting or sub-leasing the property/equipment to a third party. The ability of the deceased's estate to terminate or sublease the property will be determined by the terms of the property/equipment lease. In certain cases, the lease may automatically expire on the death of the deceased. As such, it would be a useful exercise for you to review the terms of the lease or, alternatively, engage a real estate attorney to do so on your behalf. The ultimate goal here is to reduce costs;

- terminate any hire purchase arrangements (if possible);

- cancel driver's license, magazine, newspaper and news letter subscriptions (remember some of these may be internet based – so check the deceased's credit card for clues), cable and satellite television, gym and club memberships and so on. In some cases, where these services or memberships are cancelled before expiry and have already been paid for in full it is possible to obtain refunds. Contact the relevant organization to see what their refund policy is;

- cancel all annual subscriptions and professional memberships;

- cancel health insurance, medical insurance and travel insurance coverage;

- consider whether it would be appropriate to cancel motor insurance, boat insurance, house insurance, pet insurance and any other insurance;
- cancel all credit cards and seek refunds on any gift cards;
- complete or cancel outstanding broker's orders; and
- cancel standing orders and direct debits.

Dealing With Depreciating Assets

As already mentioned, it is the responsibility of an executor to preserve the value of an estate. Hand in hand with that responsibility goes the obligation to dispose of an asset which is depreciating in value – known as a 'wasting asset'. The disposal is made to preserve the value of the asset in question.

Depreciation generally occurs where an item suffers loss in value usually due to wear, use or age. We typically think of cars as depreciating assets. Every year the car gets older and has been driven more miles it becomes a little less valuable. Houses, on the other hand, tend to appreciate in value. However, this is not always the case. For example, where a house is left vacant for a prolonged period of time it will begin to deteriorate as no one is maintaining it on a regular basis. Where this occurs, the house can be more vulnerable to vandalism in addition to the maintenance issues. In such instances, the maintenance of this house can become quite costly for the estate over time. In examples such as this, a timely sale will often place the estate in a better financial position overall.

As an executor, it will be your responsibility to identify so called 'wasting assets' – assets which are depreciating or which cost too much too maintain having regard to their value. Once identified, you should consider selling the asset. In that way, you can preserve the value of the asset in cash and eliminate the incidental costs associated with the maintenance of the asset.

However, before you go to sell the asset, you will need to review the terms of the will to ensure that you have sufficient power to dispose of the asset. Generally speaking, where you have sufficient power and the assets have not been specifically bequeathed to someone under the terms of the deceased's will, you will be free to dispose of the asset without the court's consent. However, if the assets have been left to a specific individual, you should obtain the consent of the court before selling the asset or the written consent of all beneficiaries under the will. Similarly, if you lack sufficient power under the deceased's will to sell the assets, you will also need to obtain the consent of the court before you can sell the asset.

Important Tip

Don't forget – you cannot sell or deal with the estate assets until such time as you have been formally appointed as an executor of the estate!

Securing Assets

In nearly all probate estates the deceased's assets are relatively simple to identify and therefore relatively easy to secure. They consist of such items as furnishings, clothing, jewelry, money, securities, residential and investment properties, motor vehicles and the likes. As soon as you have been issued your letters of authority appointing you as executor you can commence the task of securing these assets.

Securing the assets of the estate typically includes the following acts:-

- redirecting the deceased's mail to your address (see note above);
- arranging for the safe storage of personal valuables, assets and important legal documents. Depending on the assets in question, you may wish to consider placing the assets in a safe deposit box, bank vault or legal document vault;
- reviewing property and vehicle insurance arrangements, maintaining appropriate cover and arranging for any new or additional cover which you deem appropriate;

- if the deceased's home, office or business premises is vacant following the deceased's death, advising the insurance company of this and arranging to have someone check the property or properties regularly;
- cancelation of any un-necessary outgoings (see above);
- advising financial institutions, utilities, government bodies and associations of the deceased's death as required;
- if the deceased received benefits under a private insurance policy, contact the insurer to advise of the deceased's death and arrange payment of any sums owing under the policy. Arrange for the collection of all other benefits due to the deceased;
- if the deceased was an executor of another's estate whose administration was not complete at the time of the deceased's death, or was a trustee of a trust, you should advise the other executors or trustees (if any) of the deceased's death and, especially where there are no joint office holders, obtain professional advice as to whether you have any continuing responsibilities arising from your position as executor in respect of the other administration or trust. It's important that you take legal advice in such instances; and
- if the deceased carried on business as a sole proprietor or as the owner-manager of a corporation, then you will need to make arrangements for the continued management of the business and/or for the security of all physical assets and documents of the business. You should consider engaging professional advisors or experienced managers where you decide to carry on the business. Remember, as an executor you are required to act prudently in the management of the estate's assets. Therefore, where it is prudent to take professional advice or engage experienced personnel you should do so.

Managing Personal Property

You will need to visit the deceased's home and make an inventory list of all the deceased's tangible household personal property which will go through the probate process. If you are in any doubt as to whether particular assets will need to go through probate, contact an attorney. Turning again to the inventory, it must include a fair market value of each asset as well as details of any outstanding loans or liens against those assets. In order to determine the value of each of the assets in question, you can use the value that the property is anticipated to achieve at an auction of the estate assets. If no auction is planned, then your honest and reasonable "best-guess" estimate of value will usually be acceptable.

The level of detail required for an inventory can vary from case to case. In the ordinary course, it's acceptable to group all of the assets in to broad categories such as clothes, furniture, personal effects and the likes. However, bigger items such as vehicles and valuable antiques or jewelry should be listed separately. When valuing these 'big ticket' items, you should use an appropriate valuation method – such as a reliable trade magazine or appraiser.

As mentioned above, in certain instances the cost of maintaining assets will in fact exceed the value of the assets themselves. This of course is a situation best avoided. As such, once you have listed and valued these assets, you will need to decide what to do with them.

Where the estate is clearly in a position to discharge all creditor claims against the deceased's estate as well as all expenses and taxes of the estate, you should consider making an application to court to make an early distribution of the assets to the beneficiaries. In this way, you will shift the burden of maintaining and insuring the assets to the beneficiary and away from the estate – thereby preventing the further depletion of the estate's assets. Alternatively, you could petition the court to grant you permission to sell the asset in question – this will be required where you have no power of sale under the terms of the will. Again, as mentioned above, if the asset in question has been bequeathed to someone, you should obtain the consent of the beneficiaries before making the sale.

Managing Real Estate

Before we look at the management of real estate, it's important that you understand the different manners in which real estate can be legally held by the deceased. This will help you understand whether the real estate needs to be probated and also what you can and cannot do with it.

As indicated, whether or not the property that the deceased owned at the time of his death will need to be probated depends on how the title to that property is held. Typically, property can be held in one of four different ways:-

- joint tenancy with a right of survivorship;
- tenancy by the entireties;
- tenancy in common; and
- community property.

Joint Tenancy With a Right of Survivorship

Where a property is held under a joint tenancy, each of the property owners has an undivided percentage interest in the entire property. To illustrate this, an example is often useful. So let's, for example, take a case where four people own a property equally under a joint tenancy arrangement. Each of the four owners has an entitlement to a 25% interest in the entire or whole of the property. However, because each owner has an entitlement to a percentage of the whole, rather than having a divided and defined 25% interest in the property, he is entitled to access and take actions in respect of the entire property and not simply 25% of it.

Where a joint tenant dies, their share passes to the remaining joint tenants. Taking our example again, where one of the four property owners die, their share passes to each of the other three survivors automatically and each of the survivors then becomes entitled to a 33.33% interest in the property.

The key point to take from the above is that the share passes from the deceased joint owner to the remaining joint owners without the need for probate.

Tenancy By the Entireties

A special type of joint tenancy known as a 'tenancy by the entirety' is recognized between married couples in some states. Under this form of joint ownership, if a married couple owns property as tenants in the entirety, then each spouse must obtain the consent of the other before dealing with the property in any way that would affect the rights of the other. This includes putting in place a mortgage over the property. Each spouse lacks the power to freely dispose of their interest under their will, or in any other way, as the principle of survivorship applies between the spouses.

Did You Know?

States that recognize a 'tenancy by the entirety' include: Alaska*, Arkansas, Delaware, District of Columbia, Florida, Hawaii, Illinois*, Indiana*, Kentucky*, Maryland, Massachusetts, Michigan*, Mississippi, Missouri, New Jersey, New York*, North Carolina*, Ohio, Oklahoma, Oregon, Pennsylvania, Rhode Island, Tennessee, Utah, Vermont, Virginia and Wyoming.

*states that allow tenancy by entirety for real estate only

Tenancy in Common

A tenancy in common is one of the most common forms of property ownership in most states. A tenancy in common is created where two or more people purchase a property together as 'tenants in common'. As tenants in common, each of the parties own a separate and distinguishable part of the property. To take the example of our four property owners above, if the arrangement was a tenancy in common, each of them would own 25% of the property in their own right and would be free to sell that 25% to any person at any time and/or to dispose of their interest under their will. The right of survivorship does not apply here.

Community Property

Community property states have different rules governing probate, so it's important to understand these rules.

At the date of writing there are nine community property states namely Arizona, California, Idaho, Louisiana, Nevada, New Mexico, Texas, Washington and Wisconsin. In Alaska, couples can opt to have their property treated as community property under the terms of a written property agreement. Each of these states has special laws that dictate how married people can own and dispose property – both real and personal.

Did You Know?

Real property is property such as land, buildings and real estate generally. Personal property can be broadly defined as including all other property which a person can own.

In a community property state, the law broadly provides that all earnings generated during the course of a marriage and all property purchased during the marriage is considered community property and therefore equally owned by each spouse. Therefore if, for example, one spouse earns $100,000 per year as an executive, while the other earns $40,000 as a freelance writer, then each spouse shall be deemed to "own" $70,000 of those earnings. In addition to salary, property purchased by one spouse in his or her own name with money he or she earned during the marriage will also be regarded as community property. Similarly, debts incurred by either spouse during their marriage are regarded as debts of the couple rather than that of the individual who incurred it.

Separate property, on the other hand, includes property received by a spouse during their marriage by means of a gift or bequest under a will. It also includes any property owned by a spouse before they got married which that spouse has kept segregated from community property during the marriage. Similar to the position regarding debts above, all debts incurred by spouses prior to marriage are considered separate debts of each spouse.

Separate property can also include anything that one spouse gives up in favor of the other spouse in writing.

The distinction between community property and separate property becomes important when determining which of a spouse's assets can be freely disposed of under the terms of their will. In community property states, on the death of a spouse, half of the community property owned by the couple will go to the surviving spouse, unless the deceased spouse's will directs otherwise (i.e. provides for the transfer of part or all of their share of the community property to the surviving spouse). Otherwise, the surviving spouse is free to dispose of their share of community property as well as their separate property as they desire.

Management of Property

Now that you understand the different methods in which real estate can be held, we can look at the management of the real estate. Remember, you do not need to maintain or manage property which passes to another person as a matter of law, under a joint tenancy arrangement, at the time of the deceased's death.

As an executor, you are therefore required to maintain all other real estate owned by the deceased at the time of his or her death. This real estate includes the deceased's home, investment properties and land banks. The funds necessary to maintain the real estate can be taken from the estate's funds. In addition to discharging maintenance costs, you will also need to discharge any mortgage payments, taxes, rates and insurance premiums owing in respect of the properties in order to ensure that the properties are not placed at risk – whether from foreclosure, excessive tax penalties or otherwise.

Managing Cash Accounts and Investments

The management of cash accounts is perhaps one of the easiest of an executor's tasks. You simply need to arrange to have the proceeds of the cash account transferred to the estate bank account. In that way you will be better able to manage the proceeds and to use them to discharge debts as the need arises.

On the other hand, all non-liquid assets, such as investments, require appraisal – with the value of most securities being able to be determined easily by consulting either the Wall Street Journal or other listings and bond tables as of the date of the deceased's death. Once you have determined the value of the securities, you will need to decide whether it is prudent to hold on to the securities or liquidate them. Where the securities have been left to a beneficiary under the terms of the will, you should get the consent of the beneficiary before you dispose of the securities.

The difficulty with holding on to the securities is that their value rises and falls quite frequently. As you are obliged to take prudent steps to maintain the value of the estate's assets you may feel inclined to sell the securities as soon as possible – if the terms of the will permit. Alternatively, you may seek the court's approval to make an early distribution of the securities to the beneficiaries where there is a surplus of assets in the estate. You could even decide to hold the securities until probate has been complete in its entirety in the hope that the value of the securities might rise. In which case the securities could then be sold and applied towards the payment of debts or the proceeds distributed to the beneficiaries. However, before you decide to retain the securities, you should take proper professional advice as to the likelihood of the securities rising or falling in value – otherwise you could be held liable for a beach of your duty to act prudently and in the best interest of the estate.

Important Note

Early distributions and sale of assets...

Where the estate is clearly in a position to discharge all creditor claims against it as well as all expenses and taxes owing by it, you should consider making an application to court to make an early distribution of some of the assets to the beneficiaries. In this way, you will shift the burden of maintaining and insuring the assets to the beneficiary and away from the estate – thereby preventing the further depletion of the estate's assets. Alternatively, you could petition the court to grant you permission to sell the asset in question – this will be required where you have no power of sale under the terms of the will. Again, as mentioned above, if the asset in question has been bequeathed to someone, you should obtain the consent of the beneficiaries before making the sale.

Under the terms of a will, many executors are empowered to invest the estate funds in securities and other asset classes. However, given the nature of securities, you should be very careful as to how you invest the funds and at the very least should obtain professional advice in advance. In doing so, be mindful of the broker fees and commissions which apply.

As an alternative to investing in securities, you could always consider investing in federally insured interest bearing accounts or in government bonds. In each case, the level of risk is quite low due to fact that the government has underwritten the investments. Similar to government securities, many financial institutions offer short-term capital secure investments which you aught to consider. Remember, you must act prudently in the selection of the estate's investments – the money is not yours to risk!!

Managing a Business

The management of a business can be one of the most difficult tasks you face during the course of probating an estate. With the increased complexity associated with the management of a business comes increased responsibility to ensure that the business is properly managed. The complexity is often such that prudence would require that you engage an expert to help assess the value of the business and to assist with the operation of the business pending its sale or distribution to the beneficiaries.

Like the majority of executors, you may not have a vast degree of experience or indeed interest in running a business. As such, you may want to sell the business or turn it over to the beneficiaries under the will as soon as possible. However, if the deceased was not directly involved in the management of the business or if the business employs personnel who are capable of running the business, you may be content to allow it continue in operation for the time being.

The decision as to what happens with the business will of course be determined under the provision of the will and/or in accordance with the provisions of any agreement governing the ownership of the business such as a partnership agreement or shareholder's agreement. As an executor you should review all documents carefully to see how the ownership of the business is to be dealt with following the deceased's death. Many of these agreements provide for the valuation of the deceased's share of the business on his or her death and the subsequent transfer of his or her shares to the remaining owners of the business.

Where the will provides for the carrying on of the business, you will be permitted to do so pending transfer to the beneficiaries. On the other hand, if no provision is made, you will need to make arrangements to have the business sold or wound up. Generally, state law will stipulate a period in which the business must be wound up. Where you exceed that period, you may need to petition the court to allow extra time to facilitate the winding up.

Important Note

If you decide to carry on the business for a period of time, we recommend that you consult a lawyer to ensure that you are fully apprised of the tax, commercial and employment law issues associated with the continuance of the business.

It will not always be possible to transfer proprietary interests in professional firms such as law firms, accountancy firms or medical practices to the beneficiaries of a deceased partner. In most cases, the partnership agreement will provide for the purchase of the deceased's interest by an existing partner or an outside third party.

Sole Proprietorships

In the absence of the will providing guidance as to what should happen to a sole proprietorship owned by the deceased, you will need to determine whether it is in the best interests of the estate to close the business immediately or, with the consent of the beneficiaries, keep it in operation until it can be transferred to them. You will need to speak to the beneficiaries to determine whether they would prefer to sell or liquidate the business or maintain it as a 'going concern'.

Of course, if the estate does not have sufficient resources to meet its tax obligations or to discharge taxes, you may need to sell some or all of the business. Again, consult the beneficiaries as it may be possible to save the business by securing a loan for the purposes of paying the outstanding debts and taxes. Where a decision is made to liquidate or sell the business, you should still consider engaging a suitably qualified and experienced professional to manage the business in the short term. Remember, you are still under a duty to preserve the value of the business.

The preservation of the value of the business will be important from the point of view of ensuring that the estate gets the best possible value for the business.

In fact, in selling the business, as executor, you will be under a duty to obtain the best possible value for the business and, in due course, you may need to justify this value to the beneficiaries. It is therefore prudent to engage the services of an accountant to assist with the determination of the value of the business.

As mentioned above, you will need to carefully consider whether to maintain and manage a business pending its transfer to the beneficiaries under the will. A decision to maintain the business will normally be made in the following circumstances:

- where the will provides for the retention of the business interest without any liability to the executor (other that for fraud, willful misconduct or negligence);
- the requirement to manage the business will be for a short time only and the beneficiaries have indicated that they want to retain the business; and
- the business is making a profit and its retention does not pose an unreasonable risk to the estate.

Notwithstanding that there is in fact good reason to retain the business, certain matters need to be considered before a final decision is made. These include consideration of the following issues:

- does the executor have a good understanding of how the business operates?
- are the current management team and employees capable of carrying on the business profitably?
- is the management team trustworthy? Would it be prudent to appoint an independent person to the management team?
- are there sufficient reporting and accounting systems in place to allow the executor and the estate accountant to monitor the performance of the business?
- will the business be able to meet its obligations as they fall due?

- do the future projections for the business make it a worthwhile long term investment or would it be best to sell up now?

- are there any current or potential business liability issues? If so, are they manageable?

Partnerships

Ordinarily, under partnership law, the death of a partner dissolves the partnership, unless there is an agreement between the partners which provides to the contrary. In practice, most professional partnerships have agreements in place which regulate the transfer of partnership interests following the death of one of the partners. In most cases, in order to protect the partnership from the introduction of unwanted third parties, the partnership agreement allows the remaining partners to buy out the deceased partner's interest at a price to be determined in accordance with a valuation mechanism set out in the partnership agreement.

Where the partnership is dissolved, the surviving partners are responsible for winding up the partnership affairs and will be required to present an accounting to you as executor of the deceased partner's estate. If there is a profit on dissolution, the estate will receive its share. However, the opposite is also true. If the partnership makes a loss, the estate may need to contribute to the payment of the deceased's share of any outstanding debts.

Limited Liability Companies

Generally, where a shareholder of a limited liability company or a privately owned corporation dies, his shares will form part of his estate and he will be able to leave them as he pleases to his beneficiaries under the terms of his will or trust, as the case may be. This general rule is however subject to a number of exceptions.

It is common for shareholders in a company to enter into a shareholders agreement in order to regulate their relationship as owners of that company. Shareholder agreements typically include provisions which entitle the remaining shareholders to acquire the shares of a deceased shareholder following the death of that shareholder. In addition, these rights of acquisition or rights of first refusal are often incorporated in to the by-laws or constitutional documents of the company. The acquisition provisions typically provide a mechanism for valuing the shareholding held by the deceased shareholder and entitle the shareholders to acquire the shares from the executor or the beneficiaries at that valuation.

Where the surviving shareholders exercise their rights to acquire the deceased's shares in the company, you will only really need to concern yourself with receiving the money rather than focusing on the management of the business. Remember to verify that the surviving shareholders do have this right to buy the deceased's shares!

However, until the ownership of the shares is formally transferred, you will need to exercise the voting rights attaching to the shares. To exercise these rights to vote, you will need to formally re-register these shares in your name (as executor of the deceased's estate). The company secretary of the company can advise you as to the precise requirements in this respect.

Alternatively, if the shares are to pass to the beneficiaries under the will and there is no conflicting provision under a shareholders agreement or in the constitutional documentation of the company, you will need to consider whether to manage the deceased's interest in the business going forward or whether to sell same. In formulating your decision, the same considerations as outlined above in relation to `sole proprietorships' will apply here again.

Remember if you are in any doubt as to your rights under the terms of a shareholders agreement or under the by-laws of a company, consult an attorney experienced in this area.

Managing Debts of the Estate

As an executor, it will be your responsibility to ensure that the estate discharges all of the deceased's debts, including unpaid bills, medical expenses, funeral costs, loans and income taxes.

Having reviewed the deceased's personal belongings, mail and contacted the various financial institutions you should have a very good idea of the debts owing by the estate. Where there is a surplus of assets you should consider which debts should be paid immediately (such as mortgage and insurance payments) and which should be left on the long finger until the estate has been finalized. In the normal course, you should only arrange to make payments on behalf of the estate following your appointment as executor. However, circumstances will invariably arise where certain payments will need to be made before your appointment in order to preserve the estate. For example, a mortgage payment may need to be made to prevent foreclosure. In such cases, you should use good judgment to determine what ought to be paid in advance of your appointment and, where possible, obtain the written consent of the beneficiaries.

Remember, that you should only pay debts which are validly owing by the estate and which are enforceable against the estate. If you are in any doubt as to what is or is not validly owing, you should contact an attorney.

Before you discharge any debts, you will need to determine the precise level of debts owed by the deceased so as to ensure that the estate has sufficient money to pay them all. If there are insufficient funds to discharge the debts in full, after the sale of the assets, then you will need to pay certain debts in priority to others. In certain cases, depending on the size of the estate, you can ignore the debts completely. We will discuss the rules of priority and payment of debts in greater detail in Chapter 9 however, for the moment, it's important that you are simply aware of these matters.

Dealing With Taxes

We will discuss the precise taxes payable by the estate in more detail in Chapter 10. Having read that chapter, you can liaise with the local tax office with a view to making the necessary tax returns. You will find the IRS website quite helpful when it comes to explaining the precise returns that need to be made.

Of course, if tax computations are not your forte, you can of course engage a tax attorney or an accountant to assist with calculating any estate taxes or income taxes which are due by the estate.

More on taxes in Chapter 10.

Keep Copies of All Documents

Finally and while it might go without saying, be sure to keep copies of all records relating to the estate for at least two years following its closure. Also, keep receipts for all expenses you incurred. Remember also that as an executor you are entitled to be reimbursed from the proceeds of the estate for personal expenses incurred in settling the estate!

EXECUTOR CHECKLIST

To get a better understanding of what has to be done during probate administration, here is a checklist of duties you can use.

Duty	Due Date	Initial When Completed
File the deceased's will with court		
Inventory the deceased assets		
Open probate of the estate		
Verify insurance coverage where needed		

Duty	Due Date	Initial When Completed
Compute approximate taxes and administrative expenses		
Secure assets		
Identify creditors and pay debts		
Send notice to creditors		
Publish a notice to creditors in newspaper		
File proof of mailing and publication		
Apply for tax identification number		
Open estate bank account		
Transfer funds to estate account		
Collect life insurance		
File/mail inventory		
File the deceased's final income tax return		
Decide on estate's fiscal year		
File income tax returns for the estate		
File federal estate tax return and pay any taxes due		
File state estate tax return and pay any taxes due		
Make distributions		

Duty	Due Date	Initial When Completed
Pay administrative expenses		
Prepare final report or account		
Pay expenses of administration		
Final report or account		
File receipts for distribution		
Close estate		
Seek an order of discharge		

You'll learn more about the matters appearing in this list in the ensuing chapters.

CHAPTER 7:
PROPERTY THAT DOESN'T GO THROUGH PROBATE

Chapter Overview

Not all property passes through probate! In this chapter, we'll have a look at the various types of property that can be passed directly to beneficiaries without the need for probate.

CHAPTER 7

PROPERTY THAT DOESN'T GO THROUGH PROBATE

When Is Probate Necessary?

As you may already know, not all of a deceased person's assets need to go through probate after they die. Probate can be avoided through the use of a number of legal mechanisms including:-

(i) payable on death, transfer on death or joint accounts;

(ii) insurance policies;

(iii) joint ownership of property;

(iv) revocable living trusts;

(v) lifetime gifts; and

(vi) having property valued at or less than the limit allowed for a simplified procedure that many states allow when estates are small.

Of course, if the deceased did not provide for the transfer of all of his or her assets by means of the above methods, or indeed any of the other probate avoidance mechanisms, probate will be necessary. We'll discuss each of these probate avoidance mechanisms in more detail in the ensuing pages.

Payable on Death or Transfer on Death Accounts

One of easiest ways to avoid probate is by having pay on death (POD) and/or transfer on death (TOD) accounts. The majority of states now have laws that allow account holders to designate a named beneficiary to receive the proceeds of their bank and/or investment accounts after they have died. When the account holder dies, the money in the designated account goes directly to the named beneficiary without going through probate.

Important Note

In certain states, POD accounts are referred to as Totten Trusts after the famous New York case (In re Totten) relating to pay on death accounts.

As an executor, you should check to see if any of the deceased's accounts contain a 'POD designation'. The relevant financial institution will be able to give you information in this respect.

TOD accounts are similar to POD accounts but are more commonly used to transfer ownership of stocks, bonds and mutual funds.

Transfer on Death Securities

The Transfer on Death Security Registration Act provides for the transfer on death of stocks, shares, bonds and other financial instruments and securities. Similar to the TOD and POD accounts referred to above, these securities can be transferred on death to named beneficiaries free of the requirement to pass through probate.

To date, the following states have adopted the legislation:-

STATE	STATUS	EFFECTIVE DATE	STATE	STATUS	EFFECTIVE DATE
Alabama	*PASSED*	May 29, 1997	Montana	*PASSED*	Oct 1, 1993
Alaska	*PASSED*	Jan 1, 1997	Nebraska	*PASSED*	Sep 9, 1993
Arizona	*PASSED*	Jan 1, 1996	Nevada	*PASSED*	Jun 1, 1997
Arkansas	*PASSED*	Aug 13, 1993	New Hampshire	*PASSED*	Jun 18, 1997
California	*PASSED*	Jan 1, 1999	New Jersey	*PASSED*	Sep 20, 1995
Colorado	*PASSED*	Jul 1, 1990	New Mexico	*PASSED*	Jul 1, 1992
Connecticut	*PASSED*	May 14, 1997	New York	*PASSED*	Jan 1, 2006
Delaware	*PASSED*	Jun 26, 1996	North Carolina	*PASSED*	Oct 1, 2005
District of Columbia	*PASSED*	Apr 27, 2001	North Dakota	*PASSED*	Jul 1, 1991
Florida	*PASSED*	Jan 1, 1995	Ohio	*PASSED*	Oct 1, 1993
Georgia	*PASSED*	Jul 1, 1999	Oklahoma	*PASSED*	Sep 1, 1994
Hawaii	*PASSED*	Apr 29, 1998	Oregon	*PASSED*	Sep 29, 1991
Idaho	*PASSED*	Jul 1, 1996	Pennsylvania	*PASSED*	Dec 18, 1996
Illinois	*PASSED*	Jan 1, 1995	Rhode Island	*PASSED*	Jul 9, 1998
Indiana	*PASSED*	Jul 1, 1997	South Carolina	*PASSED*	Jun 13, 1997

STATE	STATUS	EFFECTIVE DATE	STATE	STATUS	EFFECTIVE DATE
Iowa	*PASSED*	May 26, 1997	South Dakota	*PASSED*	Jul 1, 1996
Kansas	*PASSED*	Jul 1, 1994	Tennessee	*PASSED*	Jul 1, 1995
Kentucky	*PASSED*	Aug 1, 1998	Texas	-	-
Louisiana	-	-	Utah	*PASSED*	May 1, 1995
Maine	*PASSED*	Mar 27, 1998	Vermont	*PASSED*	Jul 1, 1999
Maryland	*PASSED*	Oct 1, 1994	Virginia	*PASSED*	Jul 1, 1994
Massachusetts	*PASSED*	Nov 5, 1998	Washington	*PASSED*	Jul 25, 1993
Michigan	*PASSED*	Dec 20, 1996	West Virginia	*PASSED*	Jun 8, 1994
Minnesota	*PASSED*	Jun 1, 1992	Wisconsin	*PASSED*	May 11, 1990
Mississippi	*PASSED*	Mar 24, 1997	Wyoming	*PASSED*	Jul 1, 1993
Missouri	*PASSED*	Jan 1, 1990			

Retirement Accounts

Similar to POD accounts, it's also possible to designate beneficiaries of retirement accounts such as IRAs and 401(k)s. It's important however that this designation is made on the account documents not in the deceased's will, living trust or elsewhere. If the deceased has not complied with the relevant requirements in relation to making a designation on these accounts, the proceeds will most likely end up going through probate.

Joint Accounts

Another easy way to avoid probate is by having joint accounts. Where an account is held in the name of two or more persons and is designated with the right of survivorship, then when one of the account holders die, the surviving account holders will automatically acquire the deceased's interest in the account. Whoever is the last surviving joint owner will ultimately own the account outright.

Where a transfer occurs on survivorship, there is no need for probate. The surviving account holder will simply need to provide a copy of the deceased account owner's death certificate to the bank and the bank can then remove that person's name from the account.

The relevant financial institution should be able to advise whether the account was held with a right of survivorship designation.

Custodial Accounts

People often decide to set aside funds in the form of bank accounts, certificates of deposit or similar securities as a nest egg for their minor children, grandchildren or others, to cover things like college expenses or simply to give them a start in life. One of the most common ways of doing this is by means of a custodial account.

A custodial account is similar to a trust in many ways but is not actually a trust. With a custodial account, the proceeds or assets (where the account is an investment account) are placed under the control of a person known as a custodian. The custodian will have no beneficial interest in the account and will simply manage the account on behalf of the minor beneficiary until they reach a specified age.

It's important to note that once the custodial account is set up and the beneficiary named, the proceeds of the account then belong to the named beneficiary (usually a minor). As such, the account creator can't just take the proceeds back. Moreover, if the account generates any income that income belongs to the beneficiary (there are some exceptions to this where the account is abused to avoid tax) and tax returns may need to be made.

The account will automatically terminate when the beneficiary reaches a specified age. Almost all states have a maximum prescribed age under either the Uniform Gifts to Minors Act, 1956 or the Uniform Transfers to Minors Act, 1986.

Turning back to probate, custodial accounts will not form part of the deceased's probatable estate because the gift is deemed to have been made when the account was set up and the beneficiary named, not when the deceased died or when the custodial account terminates.

Savings Bonds

Saving bonds, like bank accounts, can be held jointly and, like POD accounts, can contain a pay on death designation. Where the deceased held savings bonds jointly, these will pass to the survivor(s) on the death of the other bond holder(s). Also, where there is a POD designation, the bonds will pass to the named beneficiary on the death of the deceased. In each case, probate will not be needed.

If the bonds are not held jointly or there is no POD designation, the bonds can only be redeemed by the executor. As such, they will form part of the deceased's probatable estate. However, the bonds may be reissued to the beneficiary under a will upon a request from the executor accompanied by a copy of the death certificate and the executor's grant of representation. As such, assuming that the estate is able to meet all its debt and tax obligations, it would be open for you to request that the bonds be re-issued in the name of the beneficiary named under the will – if there is one! Remember that this will be deemed to be an early distribution and the usual rules apply!

Life Insurance Proceeds

A life policy is another example of a simple means by which probate can be avoided. Where the deceased designated a named beneficiary under his or her life insurance policy, the proceeds of the policy which are payable on his or her death will pass directly to the named beneficiary without the need to go through probate. However, if the deceased's estate is named as the main beneficiary (which is unusual but possible) or if no beneficiaries have been named or if the named beneficiaries have died, the proceeds will need to pass to the deceased's estate and will therefore need to go through probate.

It is worth noting that where life insurance proceeds are considered to be part of the deceased's estate for probate purposes, they will also be considered to be part of the estate for federal estate tax purposes and as such will be taxable.

Joint Ownership of Property

As mentioned in Chapter 6, whether or not the property that you own at the time of your death will need to be probated depends on how the title to that property is held. Please refer to Chapter 6 for a discussion on joint ownership of property.

Revocable Living Trust

One of the most common methods used to avoid probate is to use a revocable living trust. This type of trust is established under the terms of a written trust agreement pursuant to which the creator of the trust (known as a grantor) will transfer ownership of all or certain of his personal assets into the trust. A trustee will be appointed under the agreement to hold and manage the trust assets on behalf of the trust. However, in one of the unique features of revocable living trusts, it is the grantor who is in fact appointed as trustee of the trust. In his or her capacity as trustee, the grantor can manage, invest and spend the trust property as he or she sees fit for the benefit of the grantor (himself or herself) and for the benefit of the ultimate beneficiaries of the trust. As a result, the grantor can enjoy the benefit of the trust assets in much the same way as he or she did before the assets were transferred to the trust.

As the grantor will not own the trust property in his or her individual name after the assets have been transferred into the name of the trust, the assets will not form part of the grantor's estate and will therefore not need to go through probate. When the grantor dies, the person nominated as the 'successor trustee' under the terms of the trust agreement will step into the grantor's shoes as trustee of the trust and will distribute the trust property to the beneficiaries named under the trust agreement. The whole exercise is very similar to an executor distributing assets from the deceased's estate to the beneficiaries named in the deceased's will. The big difference with living trusts however is that there will be no court supervised distribution process. Instead, the successor trustee simply abides by the instructions in the living trust.

We will discuss the settlement of a trust in more detail in Chapter 12. For the moment, just be aware that assets held in a living trust will not form part of the deceased's estate and will not need to go through probate.

Lifetime Gifts

While it may well go without saying, any property given away during the life of the deceased will not need to go through probate since anything that one doesn't own when they die does not go through probate!

Probate Free Transfers of Assets

In nearly all cases, ownership of solely owned (by the deceased) vehicles can be transferred immediately to the deceased's surviving spouse/partner or other next of kin without requiring probate, including trucks, motor homes and boats. That is if the total value of the vehicle does not exceed the amount specified under state law for such transfers. In most cases the amount will vary between $25,000 and $75,000 (depending on the laws of the deceased's state of residence).

The state Departments of Motor Vehicles can tell you whether the vehicles can be transferred without the need for probate and what needs to be done in order to carry out the transfer. Once you are in a position to legally transfer the vehicle (whether before or after probate as the case may be) the Department will, on presentation of a copy of the deceased's death certificate, transfer the title of the vehicle to the relevant beneficiary.

Note also that some states may not allow the transfer of vehicles while probate of the deceased's estate is still on-going.

In addition to vehicles, any salary, wages, accumulated vacation and sick benefits, plus any other fringe benefits, may according to the laws of certain states be paid to a deceased's surviving spouse/partner, adult children or next of kin without the need for probate. The Department of Labor should be able to tell you whether these procedures apply in the deceased's state and, if so, the deceased's employer should be able to assist you with the process generally. If you are in any doubt as to your rights or are having difficulties extracting the monies from the deceased's employer, you should contact an attorney licensed in your state.

If, for whatever reason, the vehicle or wages (as the case may be) are not transferred before probate commences, the assets may be demmed to form part of the deceased's estate and will need to go through probate. The problem with allowing this is that the spouse or next of kin may not be the beneficiaries of these items under the deceased's will. As such, they will have lost a valuable opportunity to acquire these assets and reduce the size of the probatable estate – and the related costs of probate which tend to be based on the values of the probatable estate. Any such transfers should preferable be made at the earliest opportunity.

Sample Form

Sample Form to Transfer a Motor Vehicle – State of New Jersey

(This form is used to transfer an automobile that is jointly owned between husband and wife)

STATE OF NEW JERSEY

DEPARTMENT OF LAW AND PUBLIC SAFETY

DIVISION OF MOTOR VEHICES

AFFIDAVIT

....

I, ___________________________________ undersigned, certify that I am the surviving spouse of ___________________________________.

The deceased's name,____,
and my name,____,
... appear on the certificate of ownership number _______________________
as follows:____
____

I further certify that from the time my name and the deceased's name appeared on the certificate of ownership number _________________________________until the death of the deceased on _____________________________, our relationship was husband and wife.

x____________________________

(L.S.)

Sworn and subscribed to before me on

____

____

Notary Public of New Jersey

CHAPTER 8:
HOW TO INITIATE THE PROBATE PROCESS

Chapter Overview

In this chapter, we will examine the different types of probate procedure that can be used to wind up the deceased's estate; as well as how to initiate the probate process.

CHAPTER 8

HOW TO INITIATE THE PROBATE PROCESS

What Are the Main Steps in a Probate Procedure?

Generally speaking, there are three steps in every probate proceeding:-

1. the opening;
2. the notice to creditors and estate administration; and
3. the closing.

A probate is opened by filing a petition in the probate court to have the deceased's will validated and to have an executor appointed to administer the deceased's estate. Where it is intended that the probate is to be formal (supervised by the court), there will be a brief hearing before the probate court. However, if the estate is suitable for informal (unsupervised) probate no hearing is required. We'll look at formal and informal administrations in more detail below.

The next stage is to publish a notice in a local newspaper calling for creditors to present their claims to the executor within a specific time frame. If the creditors fail to present their claims, the claims become statute barred and are unenforceable against the deceased's estate. During this notice period, the executor will be busy collecting in the assets of the estate and managing them.

Once the creditor's notice period has expired and the creditors' claims have been paid and the estate has been fully administered, the executor will close off the estate by filing the necessary documents with the probate court. Once this is done, the executor will distribute the deceased's estate to the beneficiaries named in the deceased's will or, where no will is made, to the deceased's heirs in accordance with state intestacy laws. In the same way as the opening, the closing can be formal or informal. Similarly, where there is a formal closing, a court hearing will be required. If, on the other hand, the closing is informal, no hearing will be required.

Who Can File the Petition?

Someone acting on behalf of the deceased will need to step up and submit an original copy of the deceased's will to the county probate office. As an executor, this will ordinarily be your task. Of course, if you do not wish to act as executor, the alternate executor will be entitled to make the application assuming of course that the deceased appointed one under the terms of his or her will. Failing that, the following persons will, in the following order, typically have the right to apply (1) the deceased's spouse, provided he or she is a beneficiary under the deceased's will, (2) another beneficiary under the deceased's will, (3) the deceased's surviving spouse, whether he or she is a beneficiary or not, (4) other heirs-at-law of the deceased and (5) creditors of the deceased's estate.

If, on the other hand, the deceased failed to make a will, somebody will need to petition the court to be appointed as administrator and, once appointed, the administrator will carry out a role which is virtually identical to that of the role of executor. There is of course a priority list which will determine the order in which people are entitled to assume the role of administrator (see Chapter 4). In most cases, the person appointed as administrator will be the surviving spouse or an adult child of the deceased. However, if there is any dispute over who should be entitled to serve as administrator, the probate court has discretion to determine who will be appointed and even has the power to appoint an independent public administrator to assume the role.

Where to File a Petition for Probate

Generally, the state in which the deceased lived and maintained a permanent residence at the time of death will be the state where the deceased's estate is probated and it will be the laws of that state which will govern the distribution and taxation of the deceased's estate.

Important Note

The probate court in the state in which the deceased was 'domiciled' will have jurisdiction over all of the deceased's personal property and all real estate located in that state.

While the question of permanent residence seems like a straight forward test, the determination of permanent residence can become complex where the deceased had more that one home. Where there is a question as to where the deceased permanently resided, the court will look to see where the deceased was 'domiciled'. A person's domicile is the place where he or she considered himself or herself to be from, the place to which they always intended to return or remain. While it is beyond the scope of this book to fully examine the concept of domicile, there are a number of key indicators which serve to identify where a person was domiciled. For example, where did the person spend most of their time, where does their family reside, where were they registered to vote, etc.

The determination as to where a person was domiciled is quite important in the context of probate as it determines which laws will apply to the probate or intestate administration of a person's estate. In the same way, it also serves to determine which state's tax laws will apply. These are, of course, of fundamental importance in determining the distribution of the estate and the impact of taxation on the value of that estate. By way of simple example, in certain states a spouse has a legal right to chose between the gifts left to him or her in his or her spouse's will or to take a defined portion of the deceased spouse's estate. Naturally, if a surviving spouse was left very little under the terms of his or her deceased spouse's will, they would be inclined in the case of conflict as to where the deceased spouse resided to assert that the deceased spouse resided in the state which would give the surviving spouse the greater rights to the deceased spouse's estate. The same concept applies with taxes – naturally the surviving beneficiaries of the deceased would, in the case of conflict, seek to assert that the deceased was domiciled in the state which would apply the least taxes to the estate and, more importantly, their inheritance.

Ancillary Probate

While the probate court in the state in which the deceased was domiciled (the 'home state') will have jurisdiction over (i) all of the deceased's personal property and (ii) all of the deceased's real estate located in that state, it will have no jurisdiction in relation to real estate held outside that state as state laws govern only the transfer of real estate located in that state.

So what happens when, as is fairly frequently the case, the deceased's assets include property such as a holiday home in another state? Well, in cases where the deceased owned real estate in another state, it will be necessary to carry out an ancillary probate administration in that other state in order to probate that property – assuming the property cannot be transferred by a 'small estate' procedure in that state.

An ancillary probate proceeding is a scaled-back proceeding that relates only to assets located in a particular state. In most cases, the courts in the ancillary probate state (the "ancillary state") will accept the will admitted to probate in the deceased's home state and will issue letters of authority to the executor to enable him or her to transfer the property to the beneficiary named in the deceased's will – or if there was no will, to the deceased's heirs-at-law.

As a matter of procedure, the deceased's will is first administered by the courts of the home state. Once this is done, it will then be passed on to the ancillary state or states in which the deceased owned additional real estate (including land). Assuming that the will named beneficiaries for each piece of real estate located in the ancillary state, the property will go to the named beneficiaries irrespective of which state the property is situated in or by which probate court the administration is handled.

While the probate process will take additional time where the deceased owned real estate in a number of states, a properly drafted will and an experienced probate lawyer can ensure the smooth transfer of the property to the deceased's beneficiaries. However, if the deceased failed to leave a will or left a will which failed to dispose of the property located in an ancillary state, the intestate administration laws of that ancillary state will determine the heirs-at-law who will be entitled to the property.

In relation to executors, it should be noted that while the ancillary state courts may accept the will admitted to probate in the home state, they may also require the appointment of an executor who is resident in the ancillary state. Alternatively, they may accept an executor who is resident outside the ancillary state, but in doing so may impose specific restrictions or requirements on that executor before formally allowing them to probate the assets located in that ancillary state (see Chapter 1 which mentions the position with out-of-state executors). This of course is likely to have further cost implications for the estate.

Finally, in the same way that the ancillary state's probate laws apply to the real estate located in that state so to will the tax laws. In essence, this means that any inheritance or state taxes due in respect of the probate of the real property in the ancillary state will be payable to the ancillary state and not to the home state.

How Long Will Probate Take?

The time taken for probate varies from state to state and from case to case. While many probates take less than a year, the actual time required depends on a variety of factors, including:-

- the notice period within which creditors are obliged to file claims against the estate;
- the extent, value and type of property owned by the deceased;
- how quickly the executor acts in opening and administering the probate process;
- whether the probate is formal or informal; and
- whether the deceased's beneficiaries/heirs dispute the executor's decisions or handling of the estate or even the deceased's will.

Is a Lawyer Required to Assist With Probate?

Whether or not a lawyer will be required will depend on the complexity of the deceased's estate, the type of probate being used and the laws of the state. For instances, certain states only permit lawyers to conduct legal proceedings. Therefore, a lawyer will be required where a court hearing is scheduled to take place as part of the probate proceedings.

However, for administering a small estate or for carrying out an unsupervised probate, which account for over half of all probates, there should be no need to appoint a lawyer provided of course that you are both comfortable enough and diligent enough to learn about the process on your own. Most county probate offices have guides which set out the specific requirements which need to be adhered to in the carrying out of a probate in that particular county. We recommend that you get a copy of such a guide from your county probate office before commencing with the process.

Where you chose to deal with the probate alone, the court clerk will provide you with assistance along the way. In addition, you can also hire an attorney to simply give you advice and guidance as you need it. It is important however for you to remember that most probate registrars or court clerks are not attorneys. As such their role is one of mere guidance, not the provision of advice. As such, if you come to an impasse in respect of a particular decision, you may need to turn to an attorney for advice.

Types of Probate

To "open the estate," you will need to complete and return certain probate forms to the probate office in order to notify the court, as well as other interested parties of the death of the deceased. It is at this stage, depending on state law and the size of the deceased's estate, that you may have to choose among the several different types of probate options available to you – namely (i) 'small estate' administration, (ii) unsupervised administration or (iii) supervised administration. The particular method chosen is very important as it will have a direct impact on the level of costs and time incurred in connection with the probate. We will briefly review each method below. However, if you are in any doubt as to how you should proceed and in particular which option is the best for the estate in the circumstances, you should speak to an attorney licensed in the deceased's state of residence.

Small Estates

State laws provide several alternatives to carrying out a traditional probate of an estate. When available, these methods save both time and money. They include (i) the transfers of real and personal property by affidavit and (ii) 'small estates' administration.

Small Estate Affidavit

A small estate affidavit can be used to collect a deceased's property if the combined value of all the deceased's property (excluding property that passes outside of probate), less liens and encumbrances, does not exceed a certain threshold value (which varies from state to state up to approximately $140,000). Property that can be collected with a small estate affidavit includes unpaid wages, checking and savings accounts, cars, boats, certificates of deposit, stocks and bonds. In some states, real property under a certain threshold value can be collected in the same way.

Each state sets down a specific period of time which must elapse before the small estate affidavit procedure can be used. This period can be anything right up to six months from the deceased's death, although 30 to 60 days is most common.

In each case, an affidavit will need to be completed and filed in the probate office. An affidavit is a sworn declaration that is filed with the court. Where the small estate administration procedure is applicable, the parties who are entitled to receive the deceased's assets may collect those assets by presenting an affidavit to the holder of those assets.

Certain states place limitations on who can use the procedure and some limit the procedure only to use by a spouse or child of the deceased. As such, you will need to check with the local probate court to see whether you (as executor) are entitled to avail of the procedure. If not, you may consider encouraging the deceased's spouse or children to use the procedure.

In most cases, the deceased's family can use the affidavit to collect the deceased's assets without the need to formally appoint an executor or notify the creditors of the deceased's estate. The removal of these standard probate requirements serves to make this procedure very efficient and quick.

A sample "small estate affidavit" form is contained below.

Sample Form

Sample Affidavit for Collection of Personal Property of Deceased - State of Alaska

AFFIDAVIT FOR COLLECTION OF PERSONAL PROPERTY OF DECEASED

I, [ ], being duly sworn, state the following:

1. I am the successor of ___________who died on ________, 20__. I am the successor by reason of the fact that (state basis upon which you claim to be successor).

2. The entire estate of the deceased, wherever located, less liens and encumbrances, consists only of not more than

   a. vehicles subject to registration under AS 28.10.011 with a total value that does not exceed $100,000; and

   b. personal property, other than vehicles described in (a) above, that does not exceed $50,000.

3. The deceased's estate includes no real estate.

4. Thirty days have elapsed since the death of the deceased.

5. No application or petition for the appointment of an executor of the deceased's estate is pending or has been granted in any jurisdiction.

6. I, as successor of the deceased, am entitled to the payment of any

sums of money due and owing to the deceased and to the delivery of all tangible personal property belonging to the deceased and to the delivery of all instruments evidencing a debt, obligation, stock or chose in action belonging to the deceased.

7. I understand that when I receive the deceased's assets, I am accountable for them to any executor of the estate (if one is appointed) and to any other person who has a superior right. AS 13.16.685

8. I understand I may be asked to show a copy of the deceased's death certificate to the holder of the property before any property is transferred to me.

Signature ______________________________
Mailing Address ______________________________
City state ZIP ______________________________
Telephone ______________________________

Subscribed and sworn to or affirmed before me at _____, Alaska on (date).

(SEAL) Notary Public or other person authorized to administer oaths.

My commission expires:______________________________

Alaska Statutes

Sec. 13.06.050. General definitions

(48) "successor" means a person, other than a creditor, who is entitled to property of a deceased under the deceased's will or AS 13.06 - AS 13.36;

Sec. 13.16.680. Collection of personal property by affidavit.

(a) Thirty days after the death of a deceased, any person indebted to the deceased or having possession of tangible personal property or an instrument evidencing a debt, obligation, stock, or chose in action belonging to the deceased shall make payment of the indebtedness or deliver the tangible personal property or an instrument evidencing a debt, obligation, stock, or chose in action to a person claiming to be the successor of the deceased upon being presented an affidavit made by or on behalf of the successor stating that

(1) the entire estate, wherever located, less liens and encumbrances, consists only of not more than

(A) vehicles subject to registration under AS 28.10.011 with a total value that does not exceed $100,000; and

(B) personal property, other than vehicles described in (A) of this paragraph that does not exceed $50,000;

(2) 30 days have elapsed since the death of the deceased;

(3) no application or petition for the appointment of a executor is pending or has been granted in any jurisdiction; and

(4) the claiming successor is entitled to payment or delivery of the property.

(b) A transfer agent of any security shall change the registered ownership on the books of a corporation from the deceased to the successor or successors upon the presentation of an affidavit as provided in (a) of this section. (§ 1 ch 78 SLA 1972; am § 4 ch 80 SLA 1984)

Sec. 13.16.685. Effect of affidavit.

The person paying, delivering, transferring, or issuing personal property or the evidence of it under affidavit is discharged and released to the same extent as if the person dealt with an executor of the deceased. The person is not required to see to the application of the personal property or evidence of it or to inquire into the truth of any statement in the affidavit. If any person to whom an affidavit is delivered refuses to pay, deliver, transfer, or issue any personal property or evidence of it, it may be recovered or its payment, delivery, transfer, or issuance compelled upon proof of their right in a proceeding brought for the purpose by or on behalf of the persons entitled to it. Any person to whom payment, delivery, transfer, or issuance is made is answerable and accountable for it to any executor of the estate or to any other person having a superior right. (§ 1 ch 78 SLA 1972)

Sec. 28.10.011. Vehicles subject to registration.

Every vehicle driven, moved, or parked upon a highway or other public parking place in the state shall be registered under this chapter except when the vehicle is

(1) driven or moved on a highway only for the purpose of crossing the highway from one private property to another, including an implement of husbandry as defined by regulation;
(2) driven or moved on a highway under a dealer's plate or temporary permit as provided for in AS 28.10.031 and 28.10.181(j);
(3) special mobile equipment as defined by regulation;
(4) owned by the United states;
(5) moved by human or animal power;
(6) exempt under 50 U.S.C. App. 501-591 (Soldiers' and Sailors' Civil Relief Act);
(7) driven or parked only on private property;
(8) the vehicle of a non-resident as provided under AS 28.10.121;
(9) transported under a special permit under AS 28.10.151;
(10) being driven or moved on a highway, vehicular way, or a public parking place in the state that is not connected by a land highway or vehicular way to
    (A) the land-connected state highway system; or
    (B) a highway or vehicular way with an average daily traffic volume greater than 499;
(11) an implement of husbandry operated in accordance with the provisions of AS 19.10.065;
(12) an electric personal motor vehicle

Small Estate Administration

As already mentioned, if the deceased owned few assets, it may be possible to avoid a formal probate of the estate in favor of one of the more streamlined and simplified probate procedures for what are called 'small estates'. Usually, in order to qualify for a small estate administration, the deceased's assets must be worth less than a threshold amount determined by his or her state of residence. These threshold amounts currently range as high as $200,000 in some states. In determining the value of the estate, real estate may or may not be included. This of course can have a significant impact in determining whether the small estate administration procedure can apply or not. As such, we recommend that you contact the local probate court to ascertain the thresholds which will apply in the deceased's state of residence.

This small estates procedure can be used to avoid a lengthy and costly probate administration procedure. However, in reality, as most people generally have a home or land valued over the aforementioned amounts, not everyone is able to avail of this exemption from the probate process.

While the law varies form state to state, certain states require that the deceased's creditors be paid from the deceased's assets before the small estate procedure can be used to distribute assets. You will need to check with the probate office as to the laws which apply in the state in which the probate is taking place.

Important Note

Small estate administrations vary from state to state and you will find that each state has different costs, timescales, rules, forms and regulations. Therefore, if you have any questions regarding any aspect of the small estate procedure, you will need to check with the probate court or a lawyer licensed in the state in which the probate is taking place.

To find out the correct procedure in your state for administering small estates, you should telephone the probate court and ask the clerk for the necessary form for applying for administering a small estate. These forms are also often available on the internet (see your local/state court's website) for download information. Once you obtain the form, you can fill it out, have it notarized where necessary and file it together with the deceased's death certificate and the nominal fee at the court office in order to apply to have you (or another family member of the deceased) appointed as executor of the estate. In some cases you will need to have the spouse and/or children sign their consent to your request to be appointed executor.

Once you have been authorized by the court to act as executor of the deceased's estate, you can approach financial institutions holding the deceased's assets and request that they transfer the assets to the relevant beneficiaries. In most cases, the financial institutions will require sight of your letters of authority as issued by the probate court as well as a copy of the deceased's death certificate.

The important point about this procedure is that there is generally no obligation to call on creditors to make claims against the estate (but do check the laws of your state to make certain as the laws to vary from state to state). As such, you can quickly distribute the estate assets to the beneficiaries and close the estate.

Sample Form

Sample Small Estate Affidavit – State of Washington

STATE OF WASHINGTON

Estate of:

______________________________ Small Estate Affidavit

______________________________ (RCW 11.62.010)

____

____

______________________ Deceased.

Having been sworn under oath, I declare as follows:

1. Deceased's Death Certificate. A copy of Deceased's Death Certificate is attached to this Affidavit.
2. Forty-Days Since Death. Forty (40) or more days have elapsed since Deceased's death.
3. Washington Resident. Deceased was a resident of Washington at his/her death.
4. No Executor. No application or petition for the appointment of an Executor is pending or has been granted in any jurisdiction.
5. Deceased's Net Probate Estate Does Not Exceed $100,000. The value of Deceased's entire estate subject to probate, not including any surviving spouse's community property interest in such assets, wherever located, less liens and encumbrances, does not exceed one-hundred thousand dollars ($100,000).
6. Deceased's Debts. All of Deceased's debts, including funeral and burial expenses, have been paid or provided for.
7. My Name & Address. My name and address are as shown below.

8. Claiming Successor. I am a "successor" of Deceased as defined in RCW 11.62.005.

9. Other Claiming Successors.

[ ] No Others. I am the only claiming Successor; there are no others.

OR

[ ] Other Claiming Successors. There are other claiming Successors. I have given each of them written notice, by personal service or mail, identifying my claim and describing the property claimed. At least ten (10) days have elapsed since the service or mailing of such notice

10. Entitlement to Property.

[ ] Sole Entitlement. I am personally entitled to full payment or delivery of the property claimed.

OR

[ ] Entitlement on Behalf of All Claiming Successors. I am personally entitled to full payment or delivery of the property claimed on behalf and with the written authority, of all other claiming Successors; a copy of which authority is attached to this Affidavit.

11. Property Claimed. A description of the personal property claimed, all of which is subject to probate, is as follows:

Dated: ______________________________

Signature: ______________________________

Deceased's Claiming Successor

Printed Name: ______________________________

Address: ______________________________

____

______________________________STATE OF WASHINGTON)

) ss.

COUNTY OF ________________________________)

SUBSCRIBED AND SWORN TO before me this ______ day of ___________, 200__ .

____

Signature

____

Printed Name

NOTARY PUBLIC for Washington

Residing at: ________________________________

My appointment expires on: ___________________

Declaration under Penalty of Perjury

I declare under penalty of perjury under the laws of the state of Washington that the following is true and correct to the best of my knowledge:

1. Name & Address. My name and address are as shown below.

2. Receipt of Small Estate Affidavit. I have received a copy of the Small Estate Affidavit dated, in which the Claimant declares that he/she is a Claiming Successor of the Deceased.

3. Claiming Successor. I am also a "successor" of Deceased as defined in RCW 11.62.005.

4. Authorization. I authorize the Claimant to receive full payment or delivery of the property claimed on my behalf.

5. Accounting. I am providing this authorization to the Claimant in consideration of his/her promise to me that he/she will account to me for all payments or deliveries of property received under his/her Small Estate Affidavit within five (5) business days of its receipt.

This Paragraph 5 concerns the rights and liabilities between only the Claimant and me. No possessor of any property claimed has any responsibility to see to the application of any property transferred to the Claimant.

SIGNED

Date:	On	______________________________
Place:	At	______________________________
Signature:		______________________________
		Another Claiming Successor of Deceased
Printed Name:		______________________________
Address:		______________________________
		______________________________

Generally speaking, if the deceased did not have any or much property to transfer, formal probate would not be necessary and one of the more simplified procedures would be available. However, the deceased's relatives may nonetheless decide to conduct formal probate proceedings where the deceased died owing debts and/or taxes. This is done for the purpose of ensuring a proper wind up of the deceased's estate and ensuring that creditors' claims (if any) can be properly dealt with. As you will see in the next chapter, with formal probate creditors are allocated a specific time frame within which to notify the estate of any claims that they might have against it. If a creditor fails to serve the appropriate notice within the time allocated under state law, their claim becomes statute barred. This means that the creditor will lose the right to claim against the estate if notice of the claim is not served within the allocated time frame. If a decision is made to probate an estate for these specific reasons, it would be advisable to speak to an attorney to ascertain the best options available to you.

Unsupervised Administration

An unsupervised probate proceeding is a simplified and cheaper method of probating an estate when compared to the supervised probate process (discussed below). An unsupervised probate procedure typically involves the filing of forms with the probate office, having the probate court approve the appointment of someone to wind up the deceased's estate (this may not be the executor of the deceased's will), paying any debts and taxes owing by the estate, distributing the assets to the beneficiaries named in the deceased's will and, finally, if required, having the court approve these distributions. In most instances, there will be no formal hearing or court supervision and the court's role is reduced to one of simply reviewing the paperwork filed.

Important Note

The most significant advantage of unsupervised probate is that it reduces the delay of finalization and distribution of the estate by eliminating audit and accounting reviews by the court.

The unsupervised probate process can be used for estates that exceed the monitory limits set out for small estate administration (see above) but nonetheless don't require a large degree of supervision by the courts to facilitate an orderly wind up.

The majority of states currently have procedures for unsupervised probate administration. The original intent behind the introduction of these processes was to speed up the probate process – which typically lasted a year or so. However, some states only allow unsupervised administration if all interested parties consent in advance to the procedure or if the will allows for it. Yet others, including states which have adopted the Unified Probate Code, allow the appointed administrator to commence proceedings in this way but reserve a right for interested parties to petition the court to have the proceedings converted to the traditional supervised probate process. In which case, an executor will need to be appointed and the parties will need to go through all the usual formalities associated with supervised probate.

The court has broad discretion to grant a petition for unsupervised probate, even against the deceased's wishes. Unless there is an official objection, most executors will be appointed to administer the estate without the supervision of the court, if they request it.

Factors which could cause the court to decide to temporarily or permanently carry out a formal supervised probate process include objections to the conduct or suitability of the executor, an interested party's wish to have the court review the distribution of the deceased's estate, objections to legal fees or other serious concerns about the administration.

Despite the fact that you, as administrator, may be able to avail of the unsupervised administration process, you still need to pay careful attention to the process. While the process is 'unsupervised', this does not of itself mean that you have lesser duties or responsibilities. You will still be acting as a fiduciary (a person in a position or office of trust) and, as such, you will still be held to the same high standards of conduct as would be expected of an executor. Moreover, many of the documents which must be prepared over the course of the process do not need to be filed with the probate court. Some need to be given to interested persons while others need to be filed with the court and tax authorities within specific time frames. Remember to keep careful accounting records of everything that you do with the estate in case any challenges are made to convert the procedure over to a supervised or formal probate procedure.

Notwithstanding the foregoing, one of the more positive aspects about unsupervised administration is that it can avoid (in some states) the requirement to obtain the advance approval of the court in respect of the administrator's proposed distribution of assets, the requirement to appoint and remunerate an executor and the requirement to have a final accounting. This means a saving in time and expense for everyone involved.

Even with an unsupervised probate procedure you will still need to place an advertisement in the newspaper calling for creditors to inform the estate of any monies owing by the deceased to them. Again, the creditors must notify you within a specific period of time, as set out under state law.

Sample Form

SUMMARY OF APPLICATION PROCEDURE FOR INFORMAL PROBATE IN ARIZONA

Arizona Statutes require that an executor be appointed to administer the probate. Administration of an estate includes filing a verified statement, publishing notice to creditors, giving notice as required, making distributions, filing receipts, paying taxes and closing the estate according to law.

The forms required in an ordinary probate are set out below:

Testate Estate - (Leaving a valid will)

1. Application for Informal Probate of will and Appointment of Executor **(Form PR-08)**
2. General Order to the Executor
3. statement of Informal Probate of will and Appointment of Executor **(Form PR-12)**
4. Probate Information Sheet **(PR-Cover)**
5. Letters and Acceptance of Executor **(Form PR-14)**
6. Verified statement Pursuant to A.R.S 14-5651 **(Form PR-15)**
7. Notice to Heirs and Devisees of Informal Probate and Appointment - **(Form PR-18)**
8. Notice to Creditors (You need both the forms listed below)

a. For Publication - **(Form PR-80)**

b. To known Creditors - **(Form PR-80A)**

9. Proof of Notice to Known Creditors/statement of no Known Creditors **(PR-80B)**
10. Proof of Mailing/Delivery of Inventory **(Form PR-71)**
11. Instrument or Deed of Distribution **(Form PR-101)**
12. Closing statement (You will need one of the forms listed below)
    Regular Closing statement **(Form PR-114)** or
    a.Summary Administration Closing statement **(Form PR-114A)**

Other forms may be needed in the initial filing of probate. Some of these forms include

1. Renunciation of:
    a. Right to Appointment
    b. Right to Nominate
    c. Concurrence in Nomination
    d. Waiver of Bond **(Form PR-4)**
2. Waiver of Bond **(Form PR-5)**

Intestate Estate - (Leaving no will)

1. Application for Informal Appointment of Executor **(Form PR-9)**
2. General Order to the Executor
3. Informal Appointment of Executor **(Form PR-13)**
4. Probate Information Sheet **(PR-Cover)**
5. Letters and Acceptance of Executor **(Form PR-14)**
6. Verified statement Pursuant to A.R.S 14-5651 **(Form PR-15)**
7. Notice to Heirs of Informal Appointment - Intestate **(Form PR-19)**
8. Notice to Creditors (You need both the forms listed below)
a. For Publication - **(Form PR-80)**
b. To known Creditors - **(Form PR-80A)**
9. Proof of Notice to Known Creditors/statement of no Known Creditors **(PR-80B)**
10. Proof of Mailing/Delivery of Inventory **(Form PR-71)**
11. Instrument or Deed of Distribution **(Form PR-101)**
12. Closing statement (You will need one of the forms listed below)
. Regular Closing statement **(Form PR-114)** or
  a. Summary Administration Closing statement **(Form PR-114A)**

Other forms may be needed in the initial filing of probate. Some of these forms include

1. Renunciation of:
    a. Right to Appointment
    b. Right to Nominate
    c. Concurrence in Nomination
    d. Waiver of Bond **(Form PR-4)**
2. Waiver of Bond **(Form PR-5)**

* Source: Arizona Superior court in Pima County website (http://www.**sc.pima.gov)**

Typically, a probate can be handled informally if there is an uncontested will, or in the absence of a will, if all of the heirs agree to the informal filing. If it is not possible to get the agreement of all of the heirs or if there is some kind of a dispute among the heirs, then it will be necessary to file for a formal probate.

Sample Form

SAMPLE APPLICATION FOR INFORMAL PROBATE OF WILL

AND INFORMAL APPOINTMENT OF PERSONAL REPRESENTATIVE IN COLORADO

□ District court □ Denver probate court

____ County, Colorado

court Address:

IN THE MATTER OF THE Estate OF:

Deceased

court USE ONLY

Case Number:

____

Attorney or Party Without Attorney

____

____

____

____

Division

courtroom: ____________

Phone Number: ____________ E-mail:

FAX Number: ______________

MAtty. Reg. #:

APPLICATION FOR INFORMAL PROBATE OF WILL# AND INFORMAL APPOINTMENT OF PERSONAL REPRESENTATIVE

1. Applicant, (Name) ______________________________ as __________________, is an interested person. **(§15-10-201, C.R.S.)**

2. The deceased died on the date of ______________________________, at the age of _______________ years, domiciled in the City of ____________________, County of ______________________, state of ______________________________.

3. Venue for this proceeding is proper in this county because the deceased:
□ was a domiciliary of this county on the date of death.
□was not a domiciliary of Colorado, but property of the deceased was located in this county on the date of death.

4. □ No personal representative has been appointed by a court in this state or elsewhere.
□ A personal representative of the deceased has been appointed by a court in this state or elsewhere as shown on the attached explanation. **(§15-12-301, C.R.S.)**

5. Applicant:
□ has not received a demand for notice and is unaware of any demand for notice of any probate or appointment proceeding concerning the deceased that may have been filed in this state or elsewhere.

□ has received, or is aware of, a demand for notice. See attached demand or explanation.

6. The date of deceased's last will is ________________________________ ____________________. The dates of all codicils are ____ ____.

The will and any codicils are referred to as the will. The will:
□ was deposited with this court before the deceased's death. **(§15-11-515, C.R.S.)**
□ has been delivered to this court since the deceased's death. **(§15-11-516, C.R.S.)**
□ accompanies this application.
□ has been probated in the state of ___________________________.
Authenticated copies of the will and of the statement probating it accompany this application. **(§15-12-303, C.R.S.)**

7. Except as may be disclosed on an attached explanation and after the exercise of reasonable diligence, applicant is unaware of any instrument revoking the will, is unaware of any prior wills which have not been expressly revoked by a later instrument and believes that the will is the deceased's last will and was validly executed.

8. No statutory time limitation applies to the commencement of these proceedings. **(§15-12-108, C.R.S.)**

9. ____

____

Name, address and telephone number of the nominee for Personal Representative ______________________________

____

is 21 years of age or older and has priority for appointment because of:

□nomination by the will.

□statutory priority. **(§15-12-203, C.R.S.)**

□reasons stated in the attached explanation.

Those persons having prior or equal rights to appointment have renounced their rights to appointment or have been given notice of these proceedings. **(§15-12-310, C.R.S.)** Any required renouncements accompany this application.

10. The nominee is to serve in unsupervised administration and without bond. Bond is not required by the will, nor has bond been demanded by an interested person. **(§§15-12-603 and 605, C.R.S.)**

11. The deceased □ was □ was not married at time of death.

12. Listed below are the names and addresses of deceased's spouse, children, heirs and devisees and the names and addresses of guardians or conservators of incapacitated or protected persons. (See instructions below.)

NAME (Include spouse, if any)	ADDRESS (or date of death)	AGE AND DATE OF BIRTH OF MINORS	INTEREST AND RELATIONSHIP (See instructions)

APPLICANT REQUESTS that the will be admitted to informal probate; that the nominee be informally appointed as personal representative to serve without bond in unsupervised administration; and that Letters Testamentary be issued to the personal representative.

As the applicant and being sworn, I verify that the facts set forth in this application are true to the best of my knowledge, information and belief.

_______________________________ __________

Signature of Attorney for Applicant Date

_______________________________ __________

Signature of Applicant Date

(Type or Print name, address and telephone # below)

____

____

____

____

state of ____

County of ____

Subscribed and affirmed or sworn to before me this ______day of _________________, 20 ___, by _________________________.

My commission expires: ____

____

Notary Public/Deputy Clerk

INSTRUCTIONS FOR PARAGRAPH 12:

Include any statements of legal disability or other incapacity required by Rule 10, C.R.P.P.

List the names and dates of death of any deceased devisees. (See applicable antilapse statute, **(§§15-11-601 and 603, C.R.S.)**

Where a listed person is an heir, detail the relationship to the deceased which creates heirship. Examples: son, daughter of pre-deceased son. **(§§ 15-11-101 to 114, C.R.S.)**

Attach additional sheets if necessary.

Formal or Supervised Probate Administration

A supervised probate is the most formal and expensive method of probate. In such procedures, the court plays a very active supervisory role in approving each transaction carried out by the executor. Specifically, the executor must obtain the consent of the court before selling or disposing of any of the estate assets or paying any costs or fees.

In states where it's possible to chose between supervised and unsupervised probate, a court may decide to conduct a supervised probate where:-

- the will is contested;
- an interested party requests it;
- the beneficiaries cannot agree on who should act as executor where none has been named in the will; or
- the executor's ability to carry out the process is in question.

In some states, probate proceedings can be formal in parts and informal in others. For example, the proceedings could start out on a formal basis with a court hearing being convened to appoint an executor. However, the same proceedings could end informally with papers being filed with the court detailing how the assets are to be distributed amongst the beneficiaries named in the deceased's will - rather than requesting the court to approve the distribution plan. The precise procedure for opening and closing an estate changes from state to state so you will need to check with your local probate office to confirm the rules in the deceased's state of residence.

Initiating Supervised Probate

One of the first things that should to be done following the death of the deceased is to file a copy of the deceased's will with the probate court. This should be done irrespective of whether formal probate is anticipated or not. The majority of states have under state law prescribed a particular period of time within which the will must be filed. This typically tends to be within 30 days of its discovery. However, as this time line varies from state to state you will need to check with your local probate court.

Once the will has been filed, the next step in the process will be to file a 'Petition for Probate of will and Appointment of an Executor'. This filing is made at the probate court clerk's office in the state in which the deceased resided at the time of his death and is usually made by the executor. However, it is open to anyone who has an interest in the estate (beneficiaries of the will, heirs-at-law or creditors) to lodge the petition to commence probate. Naturally no petition should be filed unless the estate actually needs to undergo probate!

The petition for probate of a will is a printed form which is generally available from the probate court, a probate lawyer, on the internet or from stationary suppliers. A sample petition is contained below.

Sample Form

SAMPLE PETITION FOR INFORMAL PROBATE OF WILL AND FORMAL APPOINTMENT OF PERSONAL REPRESENTATIVE IN COLORADO

□ District court □ Denver probate court ______________________________ County, Colorado court Address: **IN THE MATTER OF THE ESTATE OF:** **Deceased** Attorney or Party Without Attorney (Name and Address): Phone Number: E-mail: FAX Number: Atty. Reg. #:	court USE ONLY Case Number: __________ Division courtroom: __________

APPLICATION FOR INFORMAL PROBATE OF WILL AND INFORMAL APPOINTMENT OF PERSONAL REPRESENTATIVE

1. Petitioner, (Name) ______________________________ ______________________________ as __________ ______________________________, is an interested person. **(§15-10-201, C.R.S.)**

2. The deceased died on the date of ______________________ __________, at the age of __________years, domiciled in the City of ______________, County of ______________, state of ______________.

3. Venue for this proceeding is proper in this county because the deceased:
□ was a domiciliary of this county on the date of death.
□ was not a domiciliary of Colorado, but property of the deceased was located in this county on the date of death.

4. □ No personal representative has been appointed by a court in this state or elsewhere.
□ A personal representative of the deceased has been appointed by a court in this state or elsewhere as shown on the attached explanation. **(§15-12-301, C.R.S.)**

5. Petitioner:
□ has not received a demand for notice and is unaware of any demand for notice of any probate or appointment proceeding concerning the deceased that may have been filed in this state or elsewhere.
□ has received, or is aware of, a demand for notice. See attached demand or explanation.

6. The date of deceased's last will is ______________________________. The dates of all codicils are ______________________________________
____
____

The will and any codicils are referred to as the will. The will:

□ was deposited with this court before the deceased's death. **(§15-11-515, C.R.S.)**
□ has been lodged with this court since the deceased's death. **(§15-11-516, C.R.S.)**
□ is filed with this petition.
□ has been probated in the state of ______________________________
__. Authenticated copies of the will and of the statement probating it are filed with this petition. **(§15-12-402, C.R.S.)**
□ is lost, destroyed, or otherwise unavailable. See attached explanation. **(§15-12-402, C.R.S.)**

7. Except as may be disclosed on an attached explanation and after the exercise of reasonable diligence, petitioner is unaware of any instrument revoking the will, is unaware of any prior wills which have not been expressly revoked by a later instrument and believes that the will is the deceased's last will and was validly executed.

8. □ No statutory time limitation applies to the commencement of these proceedings. **(§15-12-108, C.R.S.)**
□ More than 3 years have passed since deceased's death. A statutory time limitation would apply to the commencement of these proceedings except for the circumstances described in an attachment to this petition.

9. ____

____

Name, address and telephone number of the nominee for Personal Representat

____

____

is 21 years of age or older and has priority for appointment because of:

□ nomination by the will.
□ statutory priority. **(§15-12-203, C.R.S.)**
□ reasons stated in the attached explanation.

10. The nominee is to serve:

□ without bond □ in unsupervised administration
□ with bond **(§15-12-604, C.R.S.)** □ in supervised administration

11. The deceased □ was □ was not married at time of death.

12. Listed below are the names and addresses of deceased's spouse, children, heirs and devisees and the names and addresses of guardians or conservators of incapacitated or protected persons. (See instructions below.)

NAME (Include spouse, if any)	ADDRESS (or date of death)	AGE AND DATE OF BIRTH OF MINORS	INTEREST AND RELATIONSHIP (See instructions)

PETITIONER REQUESTS that the court set a time and place of hearing; that notice be given to all interested persons as provided by law; that after notice and hearing, the court determine the heirs of the deceased and formally admit the deceased's will to probate; that the nominee:

□ be formally appointed as personal representative □ be formally confirmed as personal representative
□ without bond □ with bond
□ in unsupervised administration □ in supervised administration (additional fee required)

and that Letters Testamentary be issued to the personal representative or confirmed. Petitioner also requests:

□ a setting aside of prior informal findings as to testacy,
□ a setting aside of prior informal appointment of personal representative,
□ ____
____
____

Signature of Attorney for Petitioner Date

________________________ ______

Signature of Petitioner Date

(Type or Print name below) (Type or Print name, address and telephone # below)

____

____

INSTRUCTIONS FOR PARAGRAPH 12:

Include any statements of legal disability or other incapacity required by Rule 10, C.R.P.P.

List the names and dates of death of any deceased devisees. (See applicable antilapse statute, **§§15-11-601 and 603, C.R.S.)**

Where a listed person is an heir, detail the relationship to the deceased which creates heirship. Examples: son, daughter of pre-deceased son.

(§§15-11-101 to 114, C.R.S.)

Attach additional sheets if necessary.

* Source:- Colorado state Judicial Branch, http://www.courts.state.co.us

Notifying Interested Parties of the Hearing

Following the filing of the petition, a date will usually be set for the person named as executor (or administrator) to appear before the probate court, present the will (if you have already filed the original will with the court clerk, the clerk should return it to you upon request before the hearing so that you will have it to hand in court) and request that he or she be formally appointed as executor of the deceased's estate. This date will usually be 30 to 45 days following the filing of the petition. You should check the specific notice requirements in your state.

Note that in some states, an executor may be appointed in advance of hearing the petition to admit the will to probate without advance notice to the interested persons.

Within that period of time copies of the following must be sent to all interested persons – (a) the petition, (b) the will and (c) a written notice specifying the date, time and place of the hearing. Interested persons include all persons or entities (such as churches, charities and other organizations) named in the deceased's will, the executors named in the will (irrespective of whether they are individuals or corporations) and all persons who would be entitled to inherit from the deceased as heirs-at-law under the rules of intestate succession (even if the deceased left a valid will).

As a would-be executor, you will be obliged to make reasonable efforts to locate all interested persons. In certain states, where you fail to locate a missing person, you will be obliged to file a sworn declaration or affidavit detailing to the court the various steps you took to locate the missing person.

If the deceased is a citizen of a foreign country and he or she has died without making a will or has made a will but failed to nominate an executor, or if it appears from the terms of the will that the deceased's property will pass to a citizen of a foreign country, then you will generally be obliged to give notice of the petition to a recognized diplomatic or consular official of the foreign country where that official maintains an office in the United states.

Notice will generally be sent by first class mail or by hand to each interested person or entity at least 15 days or more prior to the hearing. This time period varies from state to state so check out the specific requirements at the local probate office, at the local library or with a local attorney. In most states, there is a specific form of notice (often called a "Notice of Petition to Administer Estate") which should be used to notify the interested persons of the petition. A copy of the form can be obtained by contacting your local probate office or visiting their website.

In certain states, you will need to have a third party serve the notices on your behalf. Where this happens, you will need to have the third party sign a sworn affidavit of service setting out details of the services. Again, you should contact your local probate office for specific details regarding the completion of this form.

Proving a Will and Dealing With Will Contests

Apart from the formal appointment of an executor, the hearing will be used as an opportunity to allow interested persons the chance to object to the will. Typical objections include assertions that the will is invalid on the grounds that:-

- it is superseded by a later will;
- it was made at a time when the deceased was mentally incompetent;
- it was made by the deceased under duress; or
- it's a forgery, either in whole or in part.

If, having reviewed the will and the circumstances surrounding the making of same, the court discovers an irregularity of some kind then it is open to the probate court, depending on the circumstances, to invalidate all provisions or only the challenged portion of the will. If the entire will is held invalid, the deceased's estate will be distributed to the deceased's heirs-at-law under the rules of the state intestacy laws.

While the petition hearing is usually routine and a lawyer's assistance is not always required, if there is a will contest – where someone disputes the validity of the will - or if there are complications, a lawyer's help will definitely be required. In many states, the probate court may require you to have a lawyer for courtroom appearances.

If questions are raised regarding the execution of the deceased's will, the witnesses may need to attend court to confirm that they did indeed witness the deceased signing the will. Alternatively, if the will has a "Self-proving Affidavit" attached to it this should be sufficient evidence to the court that the will have been executed by the deceased. A 'self-proving affidavit' is an affidavit (sworn declaration for use in court) sworn by the witnesses which eliminates the need for them to later testify in court

that they witnessed a particular person signing a will. This affidavit must be sworn before a notary public.

If it turns out that the will is in fact invalid, the deceased will be deemed to have died intestate in which case the rules regarding intestate distribution will be applied to determine how the deceased's estate will be divided amongst his or her heirs.

If, on the other hand, no objections are filed with the court and the court is satisfied with the validity of the will, it will issue an order "admitting the will to probate" and formally appoint you as executor.

Letters Testamentary

This appointment confers on you, as executor, full authority to deal with the deceased's probate estate. The court will issue you with a certified court document called "Letters of Administration" (if there was no will) or "Letters Testamentary" (where there the deceased made a will). Letters Testamentary are also known as "Letters of Authority". The Letters Testamentary are recognized by financial institutions and other parties as your official authority to deal with the deceased's estate. You will need a number of copies of the Letters Testamentary as each financial institution will want one.

Sample Form

SAMPLE LETTERS – COLORADO

□ District court □ Denver probate court _______________ County, Colorado court Address: _______________ _______________ **IN THE MATTER OF THE Estate OF:** **□ Deceased □ Protected Person Minor Ward**	**COURT USE ONLY** Case Number: Division: courtroom:
LETTERS	

(Name) _______________ *was appointed or qualified by this court or its Registrar on* _______________ *(date) as:*

□ Personal Representative. The deceased died on _______________ (date).

□ These are Letters of Administration. (The deceased did not leave a will.)

□ These are Letters Testamentary. (The deceased left a will.)

□ Special Administrator in □ an informal □ a formal proceeding. These are Letters of SpecialAdministration.

□ Conservator. These are Letters of Conservatorship.

□ The protected person is a minor whose date of birth is ____________________.

□ Special Conservator.

□ Guardian. These are Letters of Guardianship for:

□ an incapacitated person.

□ a minor whose date of birth is________________________

□ Emergency Guardian

(Expires on ____________(date), not more than 60 days after appointment per §15-14-312, C.R.S.)

Appointment or qualification is by □court order □ will □ written instrument □ ____

____

These Letters evidence full authority, except for the following limitations or restrictions, if any:____

____

Dated:__________________________ ______________________________

(Deputy) Clerk or Registrar of court

CERTIFICATION

Certification Stamp or Certified to be a true copy of the original in my custody and to be in full force and effect as of:

Dated: ___________________________________

____

(Deputy)Clerk of court

You should be aware that once a will is admitted to probate, it becomes a matter of public record as will all subsequent filings with the court. These papers are open to inspection by anyone upon payment of a small fee to the probate office. As such, it will be open to anyone who is mindful enough to inspect the will and establish who stood to inherit under the terms of that will.

The Requirements of a Surety Bond

Prior to the court appointing an executor, it may require the executor to obtain a surety bond for the estate. A bond is generally required of all executors to protect interested persons against depletion in the value of the deceased's estate arising from the wrongdoing or negligence of the executor. However, the requirement for a bond can be waived under the terms of the deceased's will or if all of the beneficiaries sign a waiver of the requirement to post bond and that waiver(s) is attached to the Petition for Probate.

Notwithstanding that there has been a waiver of the requirement to post bond, the court may decide to impose a bond if it believes that the circumstances warrant. For example, it's quite common for the court to require a non-resident executor to file a bond even where the will waives the requirement.

Where a bond is required, the amount of the bond will be calculated based on the estimated value of the deceased's estate plus the estimated value of the annual gross income of all of the estate's property. The level of bond cover can however be reduced where an executor requests the court to limit his or her authority to dealing with personal property only (such that the court's consent is required to deal with real property) or by agreeing to deposit marketable securities and/or cash not required for estate administration into a blocked account that cannot be accessed without the prior approval of the court. You will need to check your local probate rules to see whether this is permitted in your state.

In order to issue a probate bond, a copy of the court order granting probate will generally be required by the insurance companies. This order specifies the level of bond required by the court. Without this document, surety companies will often refuse to provide the bond. Failure to put a bond in place within the time frame requested by the court could lead to your non-appointment as executor or, where you have already been appointed, to your removal. You should check the specific state laws on this point.

Notifying Beneficiaries

Assuming that the will has been admitted to probate and that you have been formally appointed as an executor, the next stage of administration, after the letters are issued, is giving notice to those involved or interested in the estate. Beneficiaries will receive this required notice by certified mail; creditors by publishing a legal notice in the newspaper. We'll discuss more about creditors in the next chapter.

Collecting and Inventorying the Estate's Assets

The next steps in the process are to start collecting in the estate's probate assets and to make an inventory of these assets if you have not already done so. As you have now been issued with Letters of Authority, you will be in a position to legally call for the transfer of assets to the estate (see Chapter 6). Regarding the inventory itself, as mentioned in Chapter 6, it should be prepared within a specific time frame, usually three months. The inventory should list each item of property together with its market value at the date of death of the deceased, as well as set out details of any encumbrances registered against the asset in question. Once prepared, the inventory will need to be filed with the probate court and, if requested, sent to the beneficiaries of the deceased's estate. You will need to check the specific rules in your state to determine the time lines for filing the inventory. Once the assets are collected and the inventory is filed, the next steps in the process will be to deal with the payment of debts and taxes…..

CHAPTER 9:
CREDITOR CLAIMS

Chapter Overview

In the majority of cases, when someone passes away they will usually do so owing a number of debts - be they credit card bills or even mortgages. It is your responsibility as executor to determine which (if any) of these debts should be paid and to ensure that all claims by creditors of the deceased are dealt with in the manner prescribed by state law. We'll look at each of these matters in this chapter.

Chapter 9

CHAPTER 9

CREDITOR CLAIMS

Dealing With Creditors

Many people die leaving a large number of debts – it's almost natural. These debts can be in the form of loans, credit, taxes and hire purchase agreements; and can be either secured or unsecured. The probate process is used to ensure that all of the deceased's creditors are afforded an opportunity to recover these debts by filing a claim against the deceased's estate. All of these claims are handled through probate and, as executor, it will be your responsibility to ensure that these debts are paid in accordance with the law of the state in which the deceased was resident at the time of his or her death. In brief, you will do this by notifying the creditors of the deceased's death and of the requirement to make a claim against the deceased's estate within a specific time frame. This notification is generally made by placing a notice in a newspaper or by sending a written notice to the creditors. Once you have received details of the claims, you will then need to review each one on an individual basis and determine whether to discharge or dispute each individual claim.

There are of course some debts which it will be important to discharge as soon as possible. These include mortgage repayments, insurance premiums, utility bills and other bills which might cause the estate to lose value if not paid. As you will have already prepared an inventory of the probate assets, you should have a good idea whether the estate is solvent – that is, whether the value of the assets outweigh the value of the liabilities. If this is clearly the case, you may decide to make these payments as soon as possible in order to protect the estate. However, the payment of other debts is not something that you should rush into. You should carefully weigh up the merits of each claim before making any payment.

If the estate is insolvent, you need to be very careful in terms of how you proceed as the law sets out a specific priority in which you must pay debts (see below for further details). Remember, you can even be removed from the office of executor for improperly diminishing the value of the estate if you discharge debts which aught not to have been discharged in the circumstances.

There is a fairly procedural approach which you should take when dealing with the estate's creditors. This includes the following steps:-

- publishing a probate notice to creditors;
- conducting a review of the deceased's affairs in order to identify his or her creditors;
- giving each possible creditor actual notice in writing of the time frames within which they can make a claim against the estate;
- determining whether a creditor's claim is lawfully presented; and
- disposing of lawfully presented creditor's claims.

By adhering to the order set out above, you should be best positioned to lawfully deal with the creditors of the estate.

Identification and Notification of Creditors

Having already carried out a review of the deceased's papers and affairs in order to determine the assets and liabilities of the estate, you should have a very good idea of the debts owing by the estate. Therefore, once you have obtained your letters of authority, the first step you should take is to notify all those creditors of the deceased's death and of their entitlement to file a claim against the estate for the recovery of sums owing to them.

It's very important that you notify the creditors of their rights as soon as possible after being formally appointed. This is because, as discussed below, creditors must file their claims within a specific period of time following their notification. As such, it's important from a timing perspective to get this clock ticking as soon as possible.

Important Note

There are two different ways which a creditor can be notified of the death of the deceased and their right to claim against his or her estate – written notice delivered to the creditor or a notice in a newspaper.

In many states, the executor is required to send a written notice to all known creditors of the deceased that he or she is aware of. This written notice, which notifies creditors of the deceased's death and of their entitlement to file a claim against the estate, can be in addition to or in substitution for the publication of a notice in a newspaper. The written notice affords an additional degree of protection to the estate as once a notice is served and the affidavit of service sworn, it will be extremely difficult for a creditor to assert that he or she was unaware of the deceased's death and the need to file a claim within the required time frames.

A typical form of notice is set out on the next page.

Sample Form

<table>
<tr><th colspan="2">Sample Notice to Creditors by delivery- State of Colorado</th></tr>
<tr><td>□ District court □ Denver probate court
____
_____ County, Colorado
court Address:

IN THE MATTER OF THE Estate OF

Deceased:
Attorney or Party Without Attorney (Name and Address):

Phone Number: E-mail:
FAX Number: Atty.
Reg.#:</td><td>COURT USE ONLY

Case Number:
Division courtroom</td></tr>
<tr><td colspan="2">NOTICE TO CREDITORS BY MAIL OR DELIVERY</td></tr>
</table>

NOTICE TO CREDITORS

All persons having claims against the above-named estate are required to present them to the personal representative or the above-named court on or before ______________________________*, or be forever barred.

(date)

____

Signature of Attorney for/or Personal Representative Date

Type or Print name, of Attorney ______________________________

____

____

Type or Print name and address of Personal Representative

* Insert the later of the following two dates:

- The date set in the published Notice to Creditors by Publication (Form CPC 21-A).
- The date sixty days from the mailing or other delivery of this notice, but not later than the date one year following the deceased's death (Section 15-12-801, C.R.S.).

CERTIFICATE OF SERVICE

I certify that on (date) ______________________________, a copy of this Notice to Creditors by Mail or Delivery was served on each of the following at the indicated address by:

□ hand delivery
□ certified U.S. mail, postage pre-paid

□ first class U.S. mail, postage pre-paid
□ registered U.S. mail, postage pre-paid

Name and Address

____
Signature of Person Certifying Service

NOTE: This certificate of service cannot be used in cases where personal service is required or used. Use CPC7-P (Personal Service Affidavit) or CPC8-A (Waiver of Service) for each person required to be served personally.

However, in order to cover the situation where the deceased's personal papers failed to provide sufficient information as to the identity of all his or her creditors, it is generally required that the executor also publishes a notice of the probate proceedings in a newspaper, along with a general invitation to creditors to submit their claims to the executor within the state-specified claims period. This notice, which is often required to be published for a number of consecutive weeks, should not of course be published until you have been officially appointed as executor and received your letters of authority – otherwise, you run the risk that the notice will be held invalid. In which case you will have to repeat the process all over again and probate could be substantially delayed.

Did You Know

Publishing a probate notice to creditors immediately following your appointment as executor allows you to substantially reduce the timeframe within which a creditor can take a claim against the deceased's estate.

While the laws vary from state to state, the general requirement is that the newspaper notice is placed in at least one newspaper which is in general circulation in the county in which the probate proceedings are being held. A sample notice is set out on the next page.

Remember, the notice to creditors will also need to be filed with the probate office!

Sample Form

<table>
<tr><th colspan="2">Sample Notice to Creditors by publication - State of Colorado</th></tr>
<tr><td>□ District court □ Denver probate court
____
_ County, Colorado
court Address:

IN THE MATTER OF THE Estate OF

Deceased

Attorney or Party Without Attorney (Name and Address):

Phone Number: E-mail:
FAX Number: Atty. Reg. #:</td><td>COURT USE ONLY
Case Number:

Division
courtroom</td></tr>
<tr><td colspan="2">NOTICE TO CREDITORS BY PUBLICATION</td></tr>
</table>

NOTICE TO CREDITORS*

Estate of ____

____________________, Deceased

Case Number ______________________________________

All persons having claims against the above-named estate are required to present them to the personal representative or to

□ District court of ____,
County, Colorado,
□ probate court of the City and County of Denver, Colorado**-
on or before (date) ______________________________***, or the claims may be forever barred.

____

____

____

____

Type or Print name and address of Personal Representative

* Publish only this portion of the form.
INSTRUCTIONS TO THE NEWSPAPER:

____

Name of Newspaper

____ _______

Signature of Attorney for/or Personal Representative Date

Publish the above Notice to Creditors once
a week for three consecutive calendar weeks

____

Type or Print name of Attorney for Personal Representative

**Check whichever court applies.

***Insert date not earlier than four months from the date of first publication or the date one year from date of deceased's death, whichever occurs first

NOTE: Unless one year or more has elapsed since the death of the deceased, a personal representative shall cause a notice to creditors to be published in some daily or weekly newspaper published in the county in which the estate is being administered, or if there is no such newspaper, then in some newspaper of general circulation in an adjoining county. (§15-12-801, C.R.S.) A copy of this form and the Proof of Publication should be filed with the Clerk of the court.

Time Limitations on Submission of Claims

As already mentioned, the probate rules of virtually all states require an executor to publish, in a newspaper circulating in the county in which probate is being carried out, a notice of his or her appointment together with an invitation to creditors of the deceased person's estate to file their claims against the estate with the executor. This publication is treated as sufficient notice to creditors of the deceased's death and their entitlement to claim against the deceased's estate. More importantly however, it starts the clock ticking on the state's official claim period.

Depending upon the state in which the probate procedure is taking place, creditors of the deceased will have anywhere from three to twelve months following the date of publication to file a claim with the estate or with the probate office (depending on state law). Any claim that is notified after this period has elapsed will become statute barred and will be unenforceable by the creditor.

In the ordinary course, where a creditor files a claim following the expiry of the claim period, the executor is not required to discharge the claim. However, in certain states, the probate court has the authority to extend the claim period in exceptional circumstances; and in some instances up to three years. As such, it would be practical to take the advice of an attorney where you are seeking to deny a late claim from a creditor.

Evaluation of Claims

In most cases, having previously reviewed the deceased's papers, it will be a relatively straight forward task to identify the deceased's creditors and the amount owing to them – especially where there are clear records of same. However, matters can become more complicated where a claim is made by a creditor who is not listed in the deceased's records or where a known creditor files a claim for an amount which is different to that stated in the deceased's records. In such circumstances, you will need to examine the merits of each claim very carefully least of all because you could be held personally liable if you pay out invalid claims or if the creditors are not paid properly.

Due in part to the risk of personal liability, you will need to carefully evaluate every single claim against the deceased's estate in order to determine whether the claim is valid or not – no exceptions. Where you believe the claim to be valid, you can approve the payment of the debt – but only after you have determined whether the estate is solvent or insolvent and, if the latter is the case, applied the rules of priority set out later in this chapter.

If you do not believe the claim to be valid based on good reason, you can disallow the claim (or part of it) by filing a notice of objection or disallowance (the name of this notice varies from state to state) with the probate office. It is also open to any interested person (e.g. beneficiaries or heirs-at-law) to also file such a notice. You will need to complete this form in order to register the objection. The form usually identifies the creditor and sets out details for the rejection of the claim – whether in whole or in part. The probate office will be able to advise you of the correct form to use. A sample form for the state of Colorado is set out later in this chapter.

In addition, you will also need to send a copy of the notice of objection to the creditor by registered post. Invariably, this will result in litigation against you in your capacity as personal representative of the estate as the creditor will, in the absence of your agreement, have no other means of recovering against the estate. In which case, you may need to engage the services of an attorney licensed in the state in which the probate is taking place.

Sample Form

<table>
<tr><th colspan="2">Sample Notice of Disallowance of Claim - State of Colorado</th></tr>
<tr><td>□ District court □ Denver probate court

____
County, Colorado

Court Address:

____
IN THE MATTER OF THE ESTATE OF:

Deceased:</td><td>COURT USE ONLY</td></tr>
</table>

<table>
<tr><td>Attorney or Party Without Attorney
(Name and Address):

Phone Number: E-mail:

FAX Number: Atty. Reg.#:</td><td>Case Number:

Division:
Courtroom:</td></tr>
<tr><td colspan="2">NOTICE OF DISALLOWANCE OF CLAIM</td></tr>
</table>

TO: ____, Claimant:
Name

The undersigned, as Personal Representative of this estate, disallows

□ all of your claim
□ $ _______________________of your claim for $
_______________________ presented on
_______________________. (Date)

Failure to protest any disallowance by filing a Petition for Allowance or commencing a proceeding within sixty days after the mailing of this Notice shall result in your claim or the disallowed portion being forever barred.

____
Type or Print name of Attorney for Personal Representative

____ __________
Signature of Personal Representative or Attorney Date

____
____
____
____

Type or Print name, address & tele. # of Personal Representative

CERTIFICATE OF MAILING

I certify that I mailed a true copy of the above Notice of Disallowance of Claim to
_______________________________ Name

Claimant, on _______________________ (Date) by depositing it in the United states Mail, postage prepaid, addressed as follows:

____

____

____

____

Signature of Person Certifying Service

Similar to creditor claims, all objections against creditors' claims must also be filed within a specific time frame set out under state law. This time frame tends to be between three to four months or, alternatively, within a specific numbers of days following submission of the particular claim. Again, you will need to check the laws of the deceased's state of residence to confirm the time frames applicable in that state. Alternatively, the probate office should be able to assist you.

Payment of Claims in Solvent Estates

Once you have determined which claims are valid claims and the value of those claims, you will need to see whether there are sufficient assets to discharge these debts. If there are sufficient assets to cover the debts, the estate is said to be solvent. Where the estate is solvent you can proceed to pay the debts – but only after the claim period has expired! However, if there are insufficient liquid assets (i.e. cash) to pay the debts, you may need to sell some of the estate's assets in order to raise the money. This process is known as abatement. Unless the terms of the deceased's will specifies otherwise, the laws of the state in which the probate is being carried out will determine the order in which the deceased's estate is to be abated. A typical abatement order would be as follow:-

(i) property not disposed by the will;

(ii) residuary gift;

(iii) general money gifts from an unspecified source; and

(iv) specific gifts.

While the beneficiaries of the deceased's estate are generally not responsible for the payment of debts left by the deceased, they do in a round about way end up paying for at least some of these debts. This is because assets which would otherwise have gone to them will be taken from the estate and sold in order to pay off the deceased's debts. This has the effect of reducing the value of the estate that is left to the beneficiaries (particularly the residuary beneficiaries). They could, depending on the level of debt, potentially be left with very little or nothing at all.

Priority of Payments in Insolvent Estates

If, on the other hand, there are not enough assets to cover the payment of the deceased's debts, the estate is said to be insolvent. In cases of insolvent estates, each state has laws which govern how the assets of the estate should be distributed and, in particular, the order that creditors are to be paid.

While the order of priority varies from state to state, a representative order of priority can be seen from the uniform probate code. The code sets out the order as follows:-

(i) costs and expenses of administration;

(ii) reasonable funeral expenses;

(iii) debts and taxes with preference under federal law;

(iv) reasonable and necessary medical and hospital expenses of the last illness of the deceased, including compensation of persons attending the deceased;

(v) debts and taxes with preference under state law; and

(vi) all other claims.

If an estate is insolvent, the beneficiaries will also get nothing, even if a will leaves them specific property or specified sums of money. Beneficiaries can only receive assets in probate if there are enough assets left over after all legitimate debts have been paid.

Remember to check the laws of the state in which the probate is being administered to determine the precise payment priority in that state as the priority can change from state to state!

What Assets Should Not Be Used to Pay Debts?

It's very important to remember that, as a general rule, it only the deceased's probate assets which should be used to discharge the debts. While this general rule does not apply in the case of taxes; it nevertheless is of significance in relation to all other creditor claims.

Therefore, the proceeds of life insurance policies, pay-on-death accounts, assets owned jointly as well as assets held in a living trust need not (in many states) be used to pay debts! There is no obligation on the surviving family of the deceased to discharge any bills owing by the deceased from their own funds or from non-probate assets. The simple truth is that if there are not enough probate assets to pay all the creditors – some will just have to do without!

Finally, it's also important to note that under most state laws, the deceased's surviving spouse and minor children whom were being supported by the deceased at the time of his or her death are entitled to a reasonable allowance in money out of the estate for their maintenance during the period of administration. The family allowance is exempt from and has priority over all claims (except claims for homestead allowance). See chapter 11 for more details.

CHAPTER 10:
ESTATE TAX

Chapter Overview

In this chapter, we will look at some of the different types of taxes which may be payable following the death of the deceased. It will be your responsibility as executor to ensure that these taxes are paid by the estate.

CHAPTER 10

ESTATE TAX

Responsibilities for Payment of Tax

As the executor, administrator or personal representative of an estate, your duties will almost always include filing and paying taxes on behalf of the deceased and the estate. Alternatively, if you are a trustee of a living trust, tax liabilities that would have fallen to the estate may fall to be discharged by the trust following the deceased's death. However, where the deceased left both a living trust and probate has opened on the deceased's estate, you will not (in your capacity as trustee) generally be responsible for payment of taxes by the estate. This is because, for tax purposes, where the deceased was both the creator and trustee of a living trust that trust will be regarded as being transparent for tax purposes and will therefore still form part of the deceased's estate on death. In which case, an executor dealing with the administration of the deceased's estate should deal with the discharging of any estate tax liabilities and personal income tax liabilities. Where the probate estate is insufficient to pay the taxes, the executor may require the trustee of the living trust to contribute to the estate tax liabilities of the estate or the income tax liabilities incurred by the deceased prior to his death. Income taxes incurred after the deceased's death will be paid separately by the executor of the probate estate and the trustee of the living trust depending on whether the asset that created the income was in the estate of the living trust.

For the purposes of this chapter, we will use the term executor to encompass the roles of personal representative and trustee.

Taxes are a priority expense, meaning that they must be paid before most other creditors and certainly before any of the assets are distributed to the heirs or devisees of the estate. (As a vocabulary reminder, heirs inherit when there is no will, devisees or beneficiaries are named in the will to inherit. For the purposes of this chapter, we'll use the term heirs regardless.)

The tax maze is a complicated one, with differing taxes, deadlines and taxing authorities all in the mix. That is why most executors consult with a tax professional to ensure that all tax responsibilities are fulfilled. A certified public accountant, enrolled agent, or tax attorney will be a valuable resource to avoid making costly mistakes. When looking to use a tax professional, ask that professional about his or her experience dealing with state and federal income and estate taxes for a deceased person's estate. Some tax professionals have ample experience with living individuals and businesses, but may lack sufficient knowledge to help you with the tax requirements of an estate.

In some instances, someone else may take on the responsibility for filing certain tax returns, but you will most likely have to coordinate with that person to ensure that they pay whatever portion of the tax is owed by the estate. Remember, as an executor, the responsibility to procure the payment of taxes by the estate rests with you – and not with anyone you allow or delegate to deal with the task. By way of simple example, if you are the executor of the deceased's estate but not the surviving spouse, the surviving spouse may file the deceased's last income tax returns as part of a joint filing. Yet, paying the deceased's share of the income tax will still be the responsibility of the estate and you will be responsible to see that the estate pays it.

Note that the last sentence does not say that you must pay the taxes from your personal assets! In most situations, the executor is not required to discharge the deceased's personal taxes or indeed the estate's taxes from the executor's own funds. The money used to discharge these taxes will come from the estate – whether directly from cash held in the estate or from the proceeds of sale of the deceased's assets. In some cases, the estate may not have enough funds to pay the taxes, such as where most of the assets were held in a living trust. In those situations, the trustee and the executor (if they are different) are required to cooperate to see that the taxes are paid. The taxing authorities do not look kindly on not receiving their money, so even if there is no estate opened because everything passed outside probate, the taxing authorities expect that the person or entities that received the deceased's assets, whether through an estate, trust, or beneficiary designation, will be responsible for paying the taxes if the estate itself doesn't have enough assets to do so.

WARNING: If you, as the executor, make a payment to either a creditor or heir and then find that the estate doesn't have enough to pay the taxes you may become personally liable for payment of any outstanding taxes. This is because a presumption is raised that you failed in your duty as executor to ensure that the estate's assets are paid out in accordance with the manner and priority required by law and you must therefore bear the penalty for this - unless of course you can get the creditor or heir to give the assets back to the estate and you subsequently use them to discharge any outstanding taxes. That's why it's very important not to distribute assets to creditors or heirs until the tax liabilities are clearly determined and then only if you are very confident that distributing assets will still leave enough funds in the estate to pay the taxes.

This chapter will first address income taxes of the deceased and then income taxes of the estate. Later in the chapter, you will also read about estate, death and inheritance taxes that might be owed.

Income Taxes

Federal Income Taxes of the Deceased

As an executor, you are responsible for filing all tax returns that would have been required of the deceased were he or she alive. If the deceased had filed all his or her tax returns in a timely manner prior to his or her death, you will at a minimum have to determine if a tax return is required for the year in which the deceased died and the previous year. For example, if the deceased died in November and had filed and paid his or her taxes for the previous calendar year and all previous years, you will only be responsible for any filings required for the year in which the deceased died. However, if the deceased died in March, it is quite possible that returns had not yet been filed for the previous calendar year. In such circumstances, you will be responsible for any filings due both for the previous year and the year in which the deceased died.

Things get more complicated if the deceased failed to file required tax returns for any of the years before he or she died. You would also be required to file those in your job as executor. As a result, it is a good idea for you to check the deceased's records for at least the last three years to see if tax returns were filed. If you cannot tell from the deceased's records whether returns were filed, you may contact the Internal Revenue Service and request a transcript of the deceased's tax returns that the IRS has on file. You can request a transcript from the IRS by telephone on 1-800-829-1040, or order one by mail using IRS form 4506T (Request for Transcript of Tax Return). This form and many others are available on the IRS website at www.irs.gov.

Keep in mind that there may be no federal income tax returns required if the deceased did not have sufficient gross income. If the deceased owed any other tax, such as Medicare tax or alternative minimum tax, you will have to file a tax return regardless of the deceased's level of income. If the deceased is owed a tax refund, you will want to file a return regardless of whether it is otherwise required. To claim a refund on behalf of the deceased, you may need an extra form, IRS Form 1310 (statement of Person Claiming Refund Due a Deceased Taxpayer). Even if you determine that a federal income tax return is not required, you may decide to file an IRS form 56 (Notice Concerning Fiduciary Relationship). This form lets the IRS know that you are responsible for the estate's tax issues and you should receive any tax notices for the deceased or the estate.

The following Filing Requirement Table describes the income thresholds that require filing of a federal income tax return. The income requirements are based on the deceased's filing status, the deceased's age on December 31st of the tax year and the maximum gross income the deceased can have earned before a return is required. These numbers are current as of tax years 2009/2010 reflecting updates where applicable! Keep in mind that some income does not count towards this maximum, such as tax-exempt social security income. That is why the income of many deceased people is mainly social security may not have filed income taxes before they died and one may not be required after their death. For more on what constitutes gross income, read the instructions to IRS Form 1040.

Filing Requirement Table (Information obtained from www.irs.gov. 2010)

Deceased Filing Status	Age	Max. Income
Single	Under 65	$5,700
Single	65 or older	$7,100
Head of Household	Under 65	$8,400
Head of Household	65 or older	$9,800
Married, filing separately	Any Age	$5,700
Married, filing jointly	Both spouses under 65	$11,400
Married, filing jointly	One spouse 65 or older	$12,500
Married, filing jointly	Both spouses over 65	$13,600
Qualifying widow(er)	Under 65	$11,400
Qualifying widow(er)	65 or older	$12,500

If you determine that a tax return is required, you will need to file IRS form 1040 and any of the schedules or attachments that the Form 1040 and its instructions indicate are applicable. The Form 1040 is due on April 15th (or if the 15th falls on a Saturday or Sunday, the next business day) of the year after the end of the applicable tax year. So, if the deceased died in November, the return is due on the following April 15th. If the deceased died in March, the return for the year he died is due in about 13 months, which is April 15th of the following year. Filing extensions are allowed for up to six months, but any taxes due must be paid by April 15th even if there is an extension to file the return. See IRS form 4868 for the grounds and methods to file for an extension.

When you file the return, you will use the deceased's social security number as the tax identification number. You need to write the word "DECEASED," the deceased's name and the date of death across the top of the tax return. If filing a joint return, you should write the names and addresses of the deceased and the surviving spouse in the spaces for the names and addresses on the front of the return. If you are not filing jointly, write the deceased's name in the first space for a name on the front of the return and the personal representative's name and address in the second space (where spouse would have gone if the return was filed jointly). You will need to attach a copy of the letters of authority or other court document that appointed you as executor of the deceased's estate. The instructions that come with the IRS Form 1040 include the appropriate address to which you should mail the return based on where the deceased lived at the time of his death.

The tables that follow indicate the tax rates effective for 2010 that are applicable to individual taxpayers based on filing status. These tables have been extracted from information provided by the Internal Revenue Service at www.irs.gov.

Filing Single				
Taxable Income:		**Tax:**		
Over	But not over	Tax	+%	On amount over
$	$	$	$	$
0	8,375	0.00	10	0
8,375	34,000	837.50	15	8,375
34,000	82,400	4,681.25	25	34,000
82,400	171,850	16,781.25	28	82,400
171,850	373,650	41,827.25	33	171,850
373,650	....	108,421.25	35	373,650

Filing Jointly or Surviving Spouse of Deceased Who Died In Tax Year				
Taxable Income:		Tax:		
Over	But not over	Tax	+%	On amount over
$	$$$			
0	16,750	0.00	10	0
16,750	68,000	1,675.00	15	16,750
68,000	137,300	9,362.50	25	68,000
137,300	209,250	26,687.50	28	137,300
209,250	373,650	46,833.50	33	209,250
373,650	....	101,085.50	35	373,650

Married Filing Separate				
Taxable income:		Tax:		
Over	But not over	Tax	+%	On amount over
$	$	$		$
0	8,375	0.00	10	0
8,375	34,000	837.50	15	8,375
34,000	68,650	4,681.25	25	34,000
68,650	104,625	13,343.75	28	68,650
104,625	186,825	23,416.75	33	104,625

Married Filing Separate				
Taxable income:		Tax:		
186,825	....	50,542.75	35	186,825

Head Of Household				
Taxable income:		Tax:		
Over	But not over	Tax	+%	On amount over
$	$	$		$
0	11,950	0.00	10	0
11,950	45,550	1,195.00	15	11,950
45,550	117,650	6,235.00	25	45,550
117,650	190,550	24,260.00	28	117,650
190,550	373,650	44,672.00	33	190,550
373,650	....	105,095.00	35	373,60

State and Local Income Taxes of the Deceased

Depending on where the deceased lived and worked, you may also be responsible for filing a state income tax return in addition to the federal return. Some states charge income tax on income earned in that state even for non-residents, so if the deceased earned income from a job or business located in another state, it is important to check that state's filing requirements for non-residents. Some localities, such as counties and cities, may also require income tax. The requirements for local counties and cities are too varied for inclusion in this chapter, but can often be determined by contacting the tax collector or treasurer of the county or city.

Some states do not have an individual income tax and thus no return would be required. These states include Alaska, Florida, Nevada, New Hampshire, South Dakota, Texas, Washington and Wyoming. When an income tax return is required, it is usually due the same day as the federal income tax return (usually April 15th), but sometimes the state requirement may vary by a few days if the federal deadline fell on a weekend or holiday.

The table that follows provides information on the tax rates and standard deductions/exemptions applicable in each state. This table is created from information provided by the Federation of Tax Administrators at www.taxadmin.org.

State Income Tax Rates for Individuals For 2010 Tax Year Does Not Include Local Income Taxes				
		Standard Deduction	**Personal Exemptions**	
State	**Marginal Rates and Tax Brackets Filing Single**	**Married**	**Single**	**Dependents**
Alabama	2% > $0	$3000	$1500	$300
	4% > $500			
	5% > $3K			
Alaska	No Income Tax			
Arizona	2.59% >$0	$4200	$2100	$2300
	2.88% > $10K			
	3.36% > $25K			
	4.24% > $50K			
	4.54% > $150K			
Arkansas	1% > $0	$46 (C)	$23 (C)	$23 (C)
	2.5% > $3,700			
	3.5% > $7,400			

State	Marginal Rates and Tax Brackets Filing Single	Standard Deduction	Personal Exemptions	
		Married	Single	Dependents
	4.5% > $11,100			
	6% > $18,600			
	7% > $31,000			
California	1% > $0	$196 (C)	$98 (C)	$98 (C)
	2% > $7,168			
	4% > $16,994			
	6% > $26,821			
	8% > $37,233			
	9.3% > $47,055			
	10.3% > $1,000,000			
Conn.	3.0% > $0		Varies	$0
	5.0% > $10,000			
	3.9% > $5,000			
	4.8% > $10,000			
	5.2% > $20,000			
	5.55% > $25,000			
	5.95% > $60,000			
Delaware	2.2% > $2,000	$220 (C)	$110 (C)	$110 (C)
	3.9% > $5,000			
	4.8% > $10,000			
	5.2% > $20,000			
	5.55% > $25,000			
	5.95% > $60,000			
Florida	No Income Tax			
Georgia	1% > $0	$5400	$2700	$3000
	2% > $750			
	3% > $2,250			
	4% > $3,750			
	5% > $5,250			
	6% > $7,000			

State	Marginal Rates and Tax Brackets Filing Single	Standard Deduction Married	Personal Exemptions Single	Personal Exemptions Dependents
Hawaii	1.4% > $0	$2080	$1040	$1040
	3.2% > $2,400			
	5.5% > $4,800			
	6.4% > $9,600			
	6.8% > $14,400			
	7.2% > $19,200			
	7.6% > $24,000			
	7.9% > $36,000			
	8.25% > $48,000			
Idaho *	1.6% > $0	$7300	$3650	$3650
	3.6% > $1,237			
	4.1% > $2,474			
	6.1% > $4,987			
	7.1% > $6,184			
	7.4% > $9,276			
	7.8% > $24,736			
Illinois	3% of modified income reported on federal return	$80 (C)	$40 (C)	$40 (C)
Iowa	0.36% > $0	$1780	$40	$40
	0.72% > $1,407			
	2.43% > $2,814			
	4.5% > $5,628			
	6.12% > $12,663			
	6.48% > $21,105			
	6.8% > $28,140			
	7.92% > $42,210			
	8.98% > $63,315			
Kansas	3.5% > $0	$4500	$2250	$2250
	6.25% > $15,000			
	6.45% > $30,000			

State	Marginal Rates and Tax Brackets Filing Single	Standard Deduction	Personal Exemptions	
		Married	Single	Dependents
Kentucky	2% > $0	$40 (C)	$20 (C)	$ 20 (C)
	3% > $3,000			
	4% > $4,000			
	5% > $5,000			
	5.8% > $8,000			
	6% > $75,000			
Louisiana	2% > $0	$9000	$4500	$1000
	4% > $12,500			
	6% > $50,000			
Maine	2% > $0	$5700	$2850	$2850
	4.5% > $4,850			
	7% > $9,700			
	8.5% > $19,450			
Maryland	2% > $0	$4800	$2400	$2400
	3% > $1,000			
	4% > $2,000			
	4.75% > $3,000			
	5.25% > $300,000			
	5.5% > $500,000			
	6.25% > $1,000,000			
Mass.	5.3% /12%	$8800	$4400	$1000
Michigan	4.35% of modified income reported on federal return	$6600	$3300	$3300
Minn. *	5.35% > $0	$7300	$3650	$3650
	7.05% > $22,730			
	7.85% >$74,650			
Mississippi	3% > $0	$12000	$6000	$1500
	4% > $5,000			
	5% > $10,000			
Missouri	1.5% > $0	$4200	$2100	$1200

State	Marginal Rates and Tax Brackets Filing Single	Standard Deduction Single	Personal Exemptions Single	Personal Exemptions Dependents
	2% > $1,000			
	2.5% > $2,000			
	3% > $3,000			
	3.5% > $4,000			
	4% > $5,000			
	4.5% > $6,000			
	5% > $7,000			
	5.5% > $8,000			
	6% > $9,000			
Montana	1% > $0	$4220	$2110	$2110
	2% > $2,600			
	3% > $4,600			
	4% > $7,000			
	5% > $9,500			
	6% > $12,200			
	6.9% > $15,600			
	3.57% > $2,400			
	6.84% > $27,000			
Nevada	No Income Tax			
New	5% > $0	2400	None	None
Hampshire	(interest and dividend income only)			
New Jersey	1.4% > $0	$2000	$1000	$1500
	1.75% > $20,000			
	3.5% > $35,000			
	5.525% > $40,000			
	6.37% > $75,000			
	8.97% > $500,000			
New Mexico *	1.7% > $0	$7300	$3650	$3650
	3.2% > $5,500			
	4.7% > $11,000			

State	Marginal Rates and Tax Brackets Filing Single	Standard Deduction	Personal Exemptions	
		Single	Single	Dependents
	4.9% > $16,000			
New York	4% > $0			$1000
	4.5% > $8,000			
	5.25% > $11,000			
	5.9% > $13,000			
	6.85% > $20,000			
North *	6% > $0	$7300	$3650	$3650
Carolina	7% > $12,750			
	7.75% > $60,000			
North Dakota *	2.1% > $0	$7300	$3650	$3650
	3.92% > $32,550			
	4.34% > $78,850			
	5.04% > $164,550			
	5.54% > $357,700			
	1.174% > $5,000			
	2.348% > $10,000			
	3.521% > $20,000			
	4.109% > $40,000			
	4.695% > $80,000			
	5.451% > $100,000			
	5.925% > $200,000			
Oklahoma	0.5% > $0	$2000	$1000	$1000
	1% > $1,000			
	2% > $2,500			
	3% > $3,750			
	4% > $4,900			
	5% > $7,200			
	5.5% > $8,700			
Oregon	5% > $0	$353 (C)	$176 (C)	$176 (C)
	7% > $3,050			

State	Marginal Rates and Tax Brackets Filing Single	Standard Deduction	Personal Exemptions	
		Single	Single	Dependents
	9% > $7,600			
Penn.	3.07% > $0	None	None	None
Rhode	3.75% > $0	$7300	$3650	$3650
Island *	7% > $32,550			
	7.75%> $78,850			
	9% > $164,550			
	9.9% >$357,700			
South	0% > $0	$7300	$3650	$3650
Carolina *	3% > $2,630			
	4% > $5,260			
	5% > $7,890			
	6% > $10,520			
	7% > $13,150			
South Dakota	No Income Tax			
Tenn.	6% > $0 (interest and dividend income only)			
Texas	No Income Tax			
Utah	5% > $0	None (Credit Instead)	Varies	Varies
Vermont *	3.6% > $0	$7300	$3650	$3650
	7.2% > $32,550			
	8.5% > $78,850			
	9% > $164,550			
	9.5% > $357,700			
Virginia	2% > $0	$1860	$930	$930
	3% > $3,000			
	5% > $5,000			
	5.75% > $17,000			
Washington	No Income Tax			

State	Marginal Rates and Tax Brackets Filing Single	Standard Deduction	Personal Exemptions	
		Single	Single	Dependents
West Virginia	3% > $0	$4000	$2000	$2000
	4% > $10,000			
	4.5% > $25,000			
	6% > $40,000			
	6.5% > $60,000			
Wisconsin	4.60% > $0	$1400	$700	$700
	6.15% > $9,700			
	6.50% > $19,400			
	6.75% > $145,460			
Wyoming	No Income Tax			
Dist. Columbia	4% > $0	$3350	$1675	$1675
	6% > $10,000			
	8.5% > $40,000			

* - These states allow personal exemption or standard deductions as provided in the IRC

Federal Income Taxes of the Estate

After a death, while the deceased may not be earning income any longer, his assets may still be producing income. That income is generally paid to the estate (or the living trust if the assets were in the trust). For example, if the deceased owned stocks or other investments, any appreciation or depreciation in those investments that occurred after the date of death but before distribution to the heirs might be a taxable income or a deductible loss to the estate. Therefore, as a general rule, the estate will need to file an income tax return if it has assets that earn income or incur losses. Of course, as executor the responsibility for making this filing will fall to you.

In order to file an income tax return, the estate must have a tax identification number. The deceased's social security number is not a valid tax identification number for income or losses that accrue after the death of the deceased. To obtain a tax identification number for the estate, you must file an IRS form SS-4 (Application for An Employer Identification Number), or you can obtain a tax identification number online at the IRS website, www.irs.gov. There is no deadline by which you must obtain a taxpayer identification number, but you will need one to open a bank account and file the tax returns for the estate.

Unlike with an individual's tax return, the estate can choose its tax year, meaning that it might choose a calendar year or a fiscal year. A fiscal year can be useful if the deceased died in the middle of the calendar year, especially if the estate is able to distribute all of its assets within twelve months from the date of death. Assume, for example, that the deceased died in May and distributes its assets in April of the following year. If the estate is taxed on a calendar year, it will file one return for all of the income earned from May to December and a second return from January to April. If the estate chooses a fiscal year from May 1 to April 30, then it will only have to file one return. However, once the estate chooses its year by filing its first tax return, it cannot change to a different reporting period without getting approval from the IRS.

The estate may also choose its method of accounting, usually the cash method or the accrual method. Like the choice of accounting periods, once the estate makes its choice in its first return, it must continue to use that method for subsequent returns. If the estate's income in a taxable year is less than $600, the estate usually is not required to file an income tax return for that year. However, if the estate makes a distribution to a non-resident alien, that is, someone who is neither a resident nor a citizen of the United States, the estate must file an income tax return regardless of the amount of income.

When filing the income tax return, you will file IRS form 1041. If the estate chooses a calendar year reporting period, the Form 1041 is due by April 15th of the year following the end of the tax year. If the estate chooses a fiscal year reporting period, the form is due by the 15th day of the 4th month following the end of the reporting period. If we use our example above with a reporting period of May 1 to April 30, then the Form 1041 is due August 15th.

At the same time that you must file the IRS form 1041, you must provide an IRS form K-1 (Form 1041) to all heirs of the estate and file a copy of that K-1 with the IRS. The K-1 reports to the heir and the IRS how much of the estate's income was distributed to a particular heir. If the income was distributed to the heir, then the heir is responsible for reporting that income on his or her tax return and paying the appropriate tax on it. If the income was kept in the estate during the tax year, then the estate will pay the income tax. If an heir is a non-resident alien, you will also have to file his or her income tax return reporting the inheritance and paying the necessary tax. You use IRS Form 1040NR for that purpose.

The following table indicates the federal income tax rates applicable to trusts and estates from 2009. If you compare these rates to those applicable to individuals, you will see why it is often preferable to distribute income to the heirs and have the heirs pay tax on the income rather than keeping the income in the estate and having the estate pay the income.

Estates and Trust Federal Income Tax Rates
(This table is provided in the Instructions to IRS Form 1041)

Taxable income:		**Tax:**		
Over	**But not over**	**Tax**	**+%**	**On amount over**
$	$	$		$
0	2,300	0.00	15	0
2,300	5,350	345.00	25	2,300
5,350	8,200	1,107.50	28	5,350
8,200	11,150	1,905.50	33	8,200
11,150	.....	2,879.00	35	11,150

State and Local Income Taxes of the Estate

Depending on where the deceased lived and worked, you may also be responsible for filing a state income tax return for the estate. In some states, this will be called a Fiduciary Income Tax Return. As with individual income tax, some states charge income tax on income earned in that state even for non-residents, so if the estate earns income from an asset located in another state, it is important to check that state's filing requirements. Some localities, such as counties and cities, may also require income tax.

Most of the states that do not have an individual income tax also do not tax the income of estates. When an estate or fiduciary income tax return is required, it is usually due on April 15th of the year following the reporting year.

Estate and Inheritance Taxes

Federal Estate Tax

The federal government requires an estate to file an estate tax return whenever the value of the estate, plus any taxable gifts that were made by the deceased during the deceased's lifetime, exceeds the applicable exclusion. The exclusion amount for 2009 was $3,500,000.

The law currently provides that there will be no estate tax (and thus no requirement to file an estate tax return) if the deceased dies in calendar year 2010. However, for deceased's dying in 2011 and later, the law currently provides for an exclusion amount of $1,000,000. Although any of the laws discussed here can change at any time, the law regarding exclusion amounts is particularly likely to change. Check with your tax advisor or with the IRS to determine if the law described here is still in effect.

If the deceased left his entire estate to his spouse, there will be no estate tax due regardless of the value of the estate. However, the law still requires that the executor of the estate file an estate tax return if the estate value exceeds the exclusion amount discussed above.

The estate tax return IRS form 706 (United States Estate (and Generation-

Skipping Transfer) Tax Return) is due within nine months of the date of the deceased's death. You can receive an automatic six month extension to file the estate tax return by filing IRS Form 4768 (Application for Extension of Time To File a Return and/or Pay U.S. Estate (and Generation-Skipping Transfer) Taxes). Even if you file for an extension to file the tax return, you must still pay the estimated taxes due by the nine month deadline.

The following table applies to estates where the deceased died between January 1, 2007 and December 31, 2009. In 2010, this table would not apply because there is not scheduled to be any estate tax. In 2011 and later, this table would not apply because current law would have the tax rate return to its 2001 levels, which are higher than described here.

This table is created from information provided in the instructions for IRS Form 706.

Amount of Taxable Estate		The Federal Estate Tax	
From	**To**	**Is**	**of amount over**
$0	$10,000	18%	0
10,001	20,000	1,800 + 20%	10,000
20,001	40,000	3,800 + 22%	20,000
40,001	60,000	8,200 + 24%	40,000
60,001	80,000	13,000 + 26%	0,000
80,001	100,000	18,200 + 28%	0,000
100,001	150,000	23,800 + 30%	00,000
150,001	250,000	38,800 + 32%	50,000
250,001	500,000	70,800 + 34%	50,000
500,001	750,000	155,800 + 37%	500,000

Amount of Taxable Estate		The Federal Estate Tax	
From	To	Is	of amount over
750,001	1,000,000	248,300 + 39%	750,000
1,000,001	1,250,000	345,800 + 41%	1,000,000
1,250,001	1,500,000	448,300 + 43%	1,250,000
1,500,001	2,000,000	555,800 + 45%	1,500,000
2,000,001	& Up	780,800 + 48%	2,000,000

State and Local Estate and Inheritance Taxes

Many states impose an estate or inheritance tax. A state estate tax operates like the federal estate tax and is imposed on the estate. A state inheritance tax is a tax paid by the heirs to the estate on the amount they received as an inheritance. While you are usually required to file the return whether the tax is an estate tax or an inheritance tax, the difference between the two types of taxes affects whether the tax is applied to the entire state or proportionally among the heirs. Some local municipalities may also impose an estate or inheritance tax. For example, Nebraska does not have an estate or inheritance tax, but each county in Nebraska has an inheritance tax.

The filing deadlines for various state estate or inheritance taxes varies, but the most common deadline is the same as the deadline for filing the federal estate tax return, which is nine months from the date of death of the deceased. The following table describes the type of tax imposed and the exemption amount if the state has an estate tax. If a state is not listed in this table, it has neither an estate nor an inheritance tax. Like the federal estate tax, there is a strong possibility these laws will change in 2011.

STATE, ESTATE OR INHERITANCE TAX TABLE (As of August 31, 2010) (This table is created from information provided by various sources, including the Tennessee Department of Revenue at www.tennesee.gov/revenue the state

Tax Roundup at www.bankrate.com and CCH at http://www.finance.cch.com and other websites

STATE	TYPE OF TAX	EXEMPTION AMOUNT
Connecticut	Estate Tax	$3,500,000
Delaware	Estate Tax	$3,500,000
D. Columbia	Estate Tax	$1,000,000
Hawii	Estate Tax	$3,500,000
Illinois	Estate Tax	$2,000,000
Kansas	Estate plus Inheritance	N/A
Kentucky	Inheritance Tax	N/A
Maine	Estate	$1,000,000
Maryland	Estate plus Inheritance	$1,000,000
Massachusetts	Estate	$1,000,000
Minnesota	Estate	$1,000,000
Nebraska	Inheritance (at county level)	N/A
New Jersey	Estate plus Inheritance	$675,000
New York	Estate	$1,000,000
North Carolina	Estate	N/A

STATE	TYPE OF TAX	EXEMPTION AMOUNT
Ohio	Estate	$338,333
Oklahoma	Estate	N/A
Oregon	Estate	$1,000,000
Pennsylvania	Inheritance	N/A
Rhode Island	Estate	$ 850,000
Tennessee (seperate ingeritance tax)	Estate Plus Inheritance	N/A
Vermont	Estate	$2,000,000
Washington	Estate	$2,000,000

Note: It should be noted that many states revised the above taxes in 2010 and will continue to do so year on year! It is recommended that you research into your own states handling of estate and inheritance taxes.

CHAPTER 11:

DISTRIBUTING ASSETS AND CLOSING THE ESTATE

Chapter 11

Chapter Overview

In this chapter, we will look at the formalities associated with the distribution of the deceased's assets and how to go about closing the estate.

CHAPTER 11

DISTRIBUTING ASSETS AND CLOSING THE ESTATE

When Can I Close the Estate and Distribute the Assets?

Once all of the estate's assets have been collected and the debts and taxes have been paid, you will know what assets are left in the estate and will be responsible for the distribution of those assets to the beneficiaries named in the deceased's will or, in the case of intestacy, to the deceased's heir-at-law. However, in order to facilitate the distribution of these assets in certain states, you will first need to:

- prepare an accounting for the probate court setting out details of the financial transactions that took place during the administration of the estate; and

- petition the probate court to approve the distribution of the estate's assets in accordance with a plan submitted by you. There will usually be a short hearing to facilitate this approval.

If you are seeking compensation for your services as executor, you may need to file a petition for fees in conjunction with the petition for final distribution.

Assuming all is in order, permission should be granted to distribute the assets in accordance with the plan submitted to the court. After you have distributed the assets, the estate will be closed and you will be discharged from any further duty and potential liability as executor.

The Requirement for an Accounting

Where required, the first step in the closing process will be the preparation of an accounting. Remember of course that accountings are not required in all states and, in some states, this requirement can even be waived – so check with the probate office before you distribute any assets!

In certain states, an accounting may not be needed where all the beneficiaries entitled to receive under the deceased's will have signed a written statement either (i) waiving their right to an accounting or (ii) acknowledging that they have received their respective shares of the deceased's estate. While obtaining the latter acknowledgement will make the closing of the estate much easier, you should not attempt to close the estate in the absence of having an acknowledgement from every beneficiary – it's all or nothing here, you must have acknowledgements from all beneficiaries or you cannot avail of the shortened process!

A sample form waiving the requirement to account is set out below. Contact the probate office to obtain a copy of the form used in your state.

Sample Form

Sample Waiver of Account by Distributee - State of California

Name, Address and Telephone Number of Person Without Attorney:

____

In Pro Per

SUPERIOR COURT OF THE STATE OF CALIFORNIA

COUNTY OF SANTA CLARA

In the Matter of the Estate of) Case No.:

)

)

) WAIVER OF ACCOUNT BY

DISTRIBUTEE

)

Deceased.)

)

________________________________)

[Name] ______________________________________ [being the sole distributee/ one of the distributees] of the estate of [name] ______________________________, the deceased herein, does hereby waive the filing and settlement of a final account by [name] ______________________________ as personal representative.

Dated: _________________________ ________________________

________ (Signature)

____

(Type or print name)

Even where all of the beneficiaries waive the requirement to file an accounting, you may still be required to file a report indicating the level of compensation requested by you as executor and by the estate's attorney (if any).

Preparing an Accounting

Over the course of administering an estate, you may need to file more that one accounting with the probate office. This is because many states require the executor to produce a first accounting at the end of the first year of administration if the estate does not close during that initial year. It probably goes without saying that it's best to avoid having to prepare this initial accounting where possible. As you can imagine, the preparation of a statement outlining the financial transactions which took place in the estate over a year can be quite burdensome. Of course if the estate closes during the first year, you will only need to file a final accounting.

A final accounting will need to be filed when you are in a position to carry out a final distribution of the estate assets – i.e. after the payment of all taxes and creditors claims.

The accounting document itself is a summary of the incomes and expenditures of the estate over the course of the accounting period, with schedules attached. Once it has been prepared, it needs to be submitted to the probate court for review. If the probate court is satisfied with its accuracy, it will issue an order permitting the distribution of the remaining estate assets and discharging the executor. If, on the other hand, queries are raised in relation to the accounting, you will need to provide the relevant explanations and answers to the court. As such, while you can prepare the accounting yourself, it may make sense to engage the services of a professional to avoid the possibility of errors being discovered by the court.

A typical form of accounting is set out on the next page.

Sample Form

<table>
<tr><th colspan="2">Sample Accounting - State of Colorado</th></tr>
<tr><td>□ District Court □ Denver Probate Court
______________________County, Colorado
Court Address:

IN THE MATTER OF THE ESTATE OF:
□ Deceased □ Protected Person

Attorney or Party Without Attorney (Name and Address):

Phone Number: E-mail:
FAX Number: Atty. Reg.#:

□ INTERIM □ FINAL ACCOUNTING FOR PERIOD:</td><td>COURT USE ONLY

Case Number:

Division:
courtroom:</td></tr>
</table>

The undersigned states: That the following is a true and complete account of the administration of this estate during the period shown, both dates inclusive.

____

Signature and Title of Fiduciary

____

____

____

____

Type or print name, address & tele.# of Fiduciary

NOTE: See Rule 31 of the Colorado Rules of Probate Procedure for filing requirements and instructions.

____

SUMMARY OF CASH RECEIPTS AND EXPENDITURES ONLY

Cash Balance on hand at beginning of period of this accounting $____________________

Total cash received or collected during period of this accounting
$____________________ $____________________

Total cash paid out during period of this accounting $____________________

Cash Balance on hand at end of period of this accounting $____________________

REMARKS AND NONCASH TRANSACTIONS

CASH RECEIVED OR COLLECTED DURING PERIOD

Date	From Whom and for What:	Amount
________	________________________	________
________	________________________	________

Total Cash received or collected ________________

CASH PAID OUT DURING PERIOD

Date	From Whom and for What:	Amount
________	________________________	________
________	________________________	________

Total Cash paid out ________________

____

ASSETS REMAINING AT END OF PERIOD

Accountings typically contain the following pieces of information:-

- the accounting period covered by the accounting;
- details of the initial inventory of estate assets and the value of each asset;
- details of all income and assets received during the accounting period;
- details of all disbursements made during the accounting period;
- details of all assets currently in the executor's possession;
- a reconciliation explaining the movement of any cash balances during the accounting period; and
- any other relevant information that the court might need to know about. For example, details of any claims due, contingent expenses, advancements, investments, disposal of assets, loss of assets, etc.

In certain states, the court may request that you attach a copy of the estate bank account statement for the accounting period together with all vouchers to the back of the accounting. This assists in the validation of expenditure. Vouchers are receipts which are signed by the recipient when receiving a payment from the estate. Where required, the probate court will generally require you to submit vouchers evidencing all payments from the estate.

In addition, when submitting the accounting, you will most likely also have to include a statement indicating that all federal and state taxes have been paid.

You should check the laws of your state to determine what precisely is required to be included in the accounting. If you are in any doubt as to what to include, speak to an attorney or an accountant.

Formulating a Plan for the Distribution of the Estate Assets

Once you have prepared an accounting (assuming one is required in the state in which probate is being carried out), the next formal step is to file a petition with the court to distribute the assets of the estate. However, before filing this petition, you need to formulate a plan detailing how you intend to distribute the assets. This plan will accompany the petition.

While the plan will largely be determined by the terms of the deceased's will (assuming that the deceased died testate), there are a number of events which can have an impact, in some cases significant, on the manner in which the estate assets are to be distributed. These include:-

- ademption;
- the doctrine of lapse;
- simultaneous death;
- a spouse's right of election;
- disinheriting a child;
- homestead allowance;
- family allowance for support;
- the exemption for the benefit of the family;
- right to remain in the family home;
- right to receive family residence;
- right to automobiles;
- right to reimbursement of funeral bill;
- abatement of assets; and
- disclaimed inheritances.

We'll consider each of these further below.

Ademption

Ademption is the legal term used to describe the failure of a specific gift of an item under the terms of a will due to the fact that the item in question was no longer in the deceased's estate when the deceased died. This type of ademption is known as ademption by extinction.

In the case of specific gifts, such as the gifts of motor vehicles, jewelry, antiques and similar items of personal property, where that property has been left in a will but has actually been disposed off before the deceased's death, it is said to have adeemed. As a result of the ademption, the specific gift to the beneficiary fails. So if, for example, the deceased left his black Jaguar Roadster to his favorite nephew under the terms of his will, but before his death sold the car, the gift to the nephew would fail or be adeemed. The deceased's nephew will not be entitled to get cash or a different item of property to replace the one that was described in the will.

States that have adopted the Uniform Probate Code have attempted to abolish or scale back this common law doctrine of ademption by awarding beneficiaries certain rights where the property has been disposed of by the deceased before his death. For example, a beneficiary would, in respect of an item he was entitled to under a will be entitled to the following where the item is not in the deceased's estate at the time of death:-

(i) any balance of the purchase price owed by a purchaser to the deceased at the time of the deceased's death by reason of the sale of the specific property left to the beneficiary under the will;

(ii) certain insurance proceeds payable in respect of the asset;

(iii) any property owned by the deceased at death and acquired as a result of foreclosure, or obtained in lieu of foreclosure, of the security interest for a specifically devised obligation;

(iv) any real property or tangible personal property owned by the testator at death which the testator acquired as a replacement for specifically devised real property or tangible personal property; and

(v) in certain cases, a pecuniary devise equal to the value as of its date of disposition of other specifically devised property disposed of during the testator's lifetime but only to the extent it is established that ademption would be inconsistent with the testator's manifested plan of distribution.

Item (iv) above is quite important and is worth a more careful examination. By way of example, let's suppose that the deceased, under the terms of his will, gifted his 1954 Jaguar Roadster to his nephew as outlined above. After he had executed his will, the deceased replaced that car with a Mercedes Benz. The deceased, in turn, replaced the Mercedes Benz with an Aston Martin shortly afterwards and owned the Aston Martin at the time of his death. Under (iv) the deceased's nephew would be entitled to receive the Aston Martin in substitution for the Jaguar Roadster because it's a specific replacement item. If however, the deceased had bought stock in a mutual fund with the proceeds from the sale of the Jaguar or Mercedes, the nephew would not be entitled to the stock as it is not a specific replacement for the car – the replacement must be on a like-for-like basis.

A bequest may also be adeemed if the deceased, while still alive, gave the specific item of property to the intended beneficiary rather than waiting for the beneficiary to receive it under the terms of the deceased's will. This type of ademption is referred to as ademption by satisfaction.

A general device, on the other hand, can never be adeemed. General devices are typically gifts of cash. Where there is not enough cash in the deceased's estate to satisfy the cash gift, you may be able to sell some of the assets in the residuary estate in order to raise the necessary cash.

The Doctrine of Lapse

Ordinarily, where a potential beneficiary of a gift under the deceased's will dies before the deceased then, unless an alternate beneficiary is entitled to receive that gift, the gift to the first beneficiary lapses and reverts to form part of the deceased's residuary estate. In turn, the beneficiary of the residuary estate will receive that gift in place of the original beneficiary. This is known as the common law doctrine of lapse.

It also follows, under common law, that if the deceased beneficiary was intended to have received all or part only of the deceased's residuary estate, then in the absence of specifying an alternate to receive that gift, it would pass by intestate succession to the deceased's heirs-at-law as if the deceased made no will relating to that part of his residuary estate. It was not possible for another beneficiary of the residue estate, where there was more than one named, to take the share of the deceased residuary beneficiary as part of the overall residue. This principle was known as the "no residue of a residue" rule.

The above caused considerable difficulties for the families of deceased beneficiaries who often ultimately ended up with nothing notwithstanding that they had indirectly, through the deceased beneficiary, stood to benefit from the will maker's estate. However, the Uniform Probate Code does seek to alleviate this hardship.

A number of states, including those which have adopted the Uniform Probate Code and others, have adopted anti-lapse rules to address the situation where a gift lapses as a result of the intended beneficiary predeceasing the testator. These rules save the gift where it has been made to certain parties, usually members of the testator's family, if those family members have descendants themselves. Where this is the case, the descendants of the deceased beneficiary will inherit whatever the original beneficiary was entitled to receive under the testator's will. However, a testator can override the provisions of these anti-lapse statutes by stating in his will that the gift in question will only go to the beneficiary named in his will if that beneficiary survives the deceased, or by simply stating in the will that the anti-lapse statute does not apply. Where this happens and the beneficiary predeceases the testator, the gift will become part of the residuary estate in the usual way.

When considering whether a person survived the testator or not, it should be noted that the Uniform Probate Code provides that any devisee that dies within 120 hours of the testator's death is legally considered to have died before the testator.

The Uniform Probate Code also regulates the inheritance rights of the residuary beneficiaries where one of them dies. In particular, section 2-604(b) of the Uniform Probate Code provides that, "...if the residue is devised to two or more persons, the share of a residuary devisee that fails for any reason passes to the other residuary devisee, or to other residuary devisees in proportion to the interest of each in the remaining part of the residue". This simply means that where two or more persons (residuary beneficiaries) are entitled to the remainder of the deceased's estate and one dies then the remaining residuary beneficiaries will be entitled to receive the benefit of the deceased beneficiary's portion of the residue estate in the same percentages that they were entitled as amongst themselves to receive the remainder of the estate.

Simultaneous Death

Simultaneous death is a problem of inheritance which occurs when two people, at least one of whom is entitled to part or all of the other's estate on their death (usually a husband and wife), die at the same time in an accident. Commonly, these clauses would be used between a husband and wife as each would typically gift a large portion of their estate to the other.

In practice, wills and trusts contain survivorship clauses which provide that a beneficiary shall only be entitled to receive a gift under that instrument if they survive the will or trust maker. Additionally, it might require that the beneficiary not only survive the maker, but that the beneficiary survives the maker for a certain period of time. These types of provisions can be helpful where both parties die within a short period of time as they serve to reduce the administration costs and taxes associated with the administration of the same set of assets in two different estates. But there are even more fundamental reasons to have a survivorship clause.

The issue of who died first must be derived from all the surrounding circumstances. At common law, no assumptions are raised as to who dies first. Rather, common law requires that proof of who died first be furnished before a determination is made. As this of course created a problem where no satisfactory proof existed, various states enacted statutes to allow judges form the conclusion that that one particular person survived another under certain circumstances.

In practice, however, many of those state statutes proved inadequate. As a result, many states enacted the Uniform Simultaneous Death Act. While some slight variations exist from state to state, the law generally provides that where parties die within 120 hours of each other or in circumstances where it is not possible to determine who died first, property will be inherited and distributed as if each person had predeceased the other. This served to prevent the property from passing into the estate of a person who was already deceased, the result of which would be that the same property would need to be distributed immediately from that second estate.

Important Tip

The following states have adopted The Uniform Simultaneous Death Act:- Alaska, Arizona, Arkansas, Colorado, District of Columbia, Hawaii, Kansas, Kentucky, Montana, New Hampshire, New Mexico, North Carolina, North Dakota, Ohio, Oregon, South Dakota, Utah, Virginia and Wisconsin.

It's worth pointing out that the Simultaneous Death Act will not apply where evidence is available to demonstrate that one person survived the other. The Act will only apply where it cannot be readily determined who died first. Also, the Act will not apply if a will includes its own survivorship requirements as the survivorship requirements set out in the will serve to override what is contained in the Act.

By way of example, consider the case of Mark and Alison, a married couple with no children. They die in a car accident in circumstances where it cannot be ascertained who died first. Neither of them had executed a will so both of their families claim their assets. In such circumstances, they will look to the Uniform Simultaneous Death Act to help resolve the dispute. Under the provisions of the Act, Mark is deemed to have predeceased Alison, but Alison is also considered to have predeceased Mark. The inheritance is divided equally among their closest living relatives, according to the rules of intestacy. The same result would apply if Alison died 100 hours after Mark as she failed to survive Mark by the required 120 hours under the Act. However, if Alison dies 140 hours after Mark, matters will change substantially as Alison's estate will be entitled to claim the share of Mark's estate that Alison would have been entitled to had she ultimately survived Mark.

As an executor, you will need to carefully check the rules regarding survivorship in the deceased's state of residence if alternative requirements are not set out in the deceased's will and both the deceased and a beneficiary under the will die within a very short space of time.

A Spouse's Right of Election

The laws of most states allow a surviving spouse the choice of choosing between what he or she has been left under the terms of their deceased spouse's will or receiving a specific share of the deceased spouse's estate as defined by statute. This share is known as the minimum or "elective" share. While the amount of this share tends to vary from state to state, the general rule is that if the deceased spouse had no children the surviving spouse would be entitled to half of the deceased spouse's net estate. On the other hand, where the deceased spouse had children, the surviving spouse will have an entitlement to claim one third of the deceased spouse's net estate. Some states also impose financial thresholds. For example, under New York law, a surviving souse is entitled to $50,000 or one third of the deceased spouse's net estate, whichever is the greater.

Important Tip

Divorce terminates the right of election by the surviving spouse.

Where the deceased spouse leaves more than the elective share of the net estate to the surviving spouse, the surviving spouse would generally not exercise the right of election unless he or she felt it was more advantageous to allow a greater part of the deceased spouse's estate to pass to the other beneficiaries named in the will, for tax reasons or otherwise. Of course, the spouse's right of election is really only valuable where the deceased spouse left less than the elective share of his or her net estate to the surviving spouse. Consider, for example, the situation where a husband dies leaving everything to his children. In such a case, the surviving spouse would under New York law, for example, have the right to receive the elective share (i.e., the greater of $50,000 or one-third of the estate) notwithstanding the terms of the deceased spouse's will. The consequence of this is that the amount of the deceased's estate passing to the beneficiaries named in the will would be reduced. It may even be the case that certain legacies and gifts may abate or be adeemed in order to satisfy the spouse's elective share.

If a surviving spouse elects to take his or her legal share rather than take what was left to them under the terms of the deceased spouse's will, then he or she generally forfeits the right to receive anything under the will. That said, in many cases where the election is made, the spouse will often be allowed take some or all of the items (depending on what was gifted to the surviving spouse) left to them under the will particularly in circumstances where the amount left under the will is in fact less than the spouse's elective share. The balance of any amount owing to the surviving spouse is often then made up in cash. Alternatively, he or she can take assets from the residuary estate (in the same way as ademption operates) and so on until the legal share is satisfied. On the other hand, if the spouse elects to take his or her inheritance under their former spouse's will, he or she will generally be entitled (in the absence of abatement or ademption) to receive only those assets from the estate.

Whatever choice a surviving spouse makes, it's important to remember that they will (unless the terms of the will provides otherwise) still be entitled to avail of their other legal rights which, depending on the state law, include the right to buy certain estate assets, to remain in the principal residence for a specific period of time (usually a year), to claim and receive an allowance for their support, to receive automobiles and watercraft owned by the deceased and to avail of such other rights as a surviving spouse would ordinarily be entitled to under law.

While in most cases, the election of the surviving spouse will not affect certain non-probate property, such as jointly owned property and property with rights of survivorship attached, pay-on-death accounts and transfer-on-death securities, it may well have an effect on other types of non-probate property such as property held in a trust. That said, in states which have adopted the Uniform Probate Code, certain assets which passed to the surviving spouse either during the life of the deceased spouse or on the death of the deceased spouse (thorough joint tenancy or on survivorship) can be deemed to form part of the surviving spouse's elective share. You will need to check the laws of the deceased's state of residence to determine the precise rules in this respect.

Where a surviving spouse elects to take his or her elective share instead of any gifts made to them under the deceased spouse's will, the executor will need to construe the will as if the additional property taken by the surviving spouse had in fact been disposed of before the deceased's death. As a result, the rules of abatement will apply.

Important Note

The decision by a surviving spouse to take his or her elective share should generally be in writing and should be signed and acknowledged by the surviving spouse. Where the surviving spouse is legally incompetent, the election should be signed by the surviving spouse's guardian or conservator. Once signed, a copy of the election should be filed with the probate court clerk. Thereafter, the clerk will often send a copy of the written election to the executor.

While the law varies from state to state, a spouse who wishes to take his or her elective share can do so in writing or by appearing before the probate court. In some cases, the right can be exercised by taking no action at all. Whatever the requirements are for an effective election in the deceased's state of residence, you will need to ensure that the election is made within the time frames set out under state law. This tends to be between one to six months from the date of appointment of the initial executor to an estate although the time period can be extended where there is ongoing litigation in relation to the will. An executor is often required to notify the surviving spouse of his or her legal right to claim an elective share and many states have specific forms for such notification which also contain a relatively detailed synopsis of that legal right. Remember, if the election is not made, the surviving spouse's right of election is generally forfeited.

As you will have gathered from the foregoing, in most states, the deceased cannot simply disinherit his or her spouse. This is also the case in community property states where a surviving spouse is generally entitled to half of the couple's community property irrespective of the terms of the deceased spouse's will. If you are in any doubt as to the rights of the surviving spouse in the deceased's state of residence, we recommend that you consult an attorney.

Important Note

If a spouse wishes to claim an elective share, he or she must do so in writing within a specific time frame.

Disinheriting a Child

Unlike the position in relation to spouses, it is possible to completely disinherit children in virtually every state in the U.S. Only in Louisiana is this restricted. This can be done if the deceased's will (i) expressly states that the deceased intended to disinherit a child or (ii) makes only a nominal gift to a child (such as a gift of $10). If the deceased's will fails to mention all or any of the deceased's children as aforesaid, it would be open for any child which has not been mentioned to challenge the deceased's will and to possibly obtain a large portion of the deceased's estate as a result and in some cases an amount equal to what the child would have received had the deceased died intestate (without having made a will).

Moreover, in some states, the above laws apply not only to children of the deceased but also to their grandchildren. This, in essence, allows grandchildren to challenge the will of a grandparent who failed to provide for them or their dead parent. As such, in order for the deceased to successfully disinherit a grandchild, they would need to ensure that the grandchild is expressly disinherited in the same way as mentioned above in relation to the deceased's children.

In certain circumstances however children are entitled to claim a share of a deceased parent's property, regardless of the terms of their parent's will. For example, if the deceased lived in the state of Florida and was the head of their family for tax purposes, they would be prohibited from leaving their home to anyone besides their spouse or children.

Where any questions arise in relation to the disinheritance of a child you should consult an attorney. Remember, the estate will bear the cost of these legal fees not you personally!

Homestead Allowance

In all states, a deceased's surviving spouse is entitled to receive a homestead allowance from the deceased spouse's estate. The amount of this allowance varies from state to state and in some cases is dependent on the value of the deceased's estate. While the Uniform Probate Code suggests a figure of $15,000 for this allowance, it leaves it up to the discretion of each adopting state to determine the precise amount of the allowance.

Under the Uniform Probate Code, where the deceased's spouse has predeceased the deceased, each minor child and each dependent child of the deceased shall be entitled to a homestead allowance amounting in such amount as determined by the relevant adoptee state divided by the number of minor and dependent children of the deceased. The homestead allowance is exempt from and has priority over all claims against the estate. Homestead allowance is in addition to any share of the deceased's estate passing to the surviving spouse or minor or dependent child under the deceased's will (unless otherwise provided in the will), by intestate succession or by way of elective share.

Important Note

If a spouse or child wishes to claim the homestead allowance, he or she may be required under state law do so in writing within a specific time frame. In addition, he or she may need to survive the deceased spouse/parent by a specific number of days depending on state law.

Family Allowance for Support

In addition, the deceased's surviving spouse and dependent children are also entitled to an allowance in money out of the deceased's estate for their maintenance during the period of administration. The amount varies from state to state. Under the Uniform Probate Code, the amount payable is to be reasonable having regard to the previous standard of living and other financial resources available to the family members. In other states, the amount is limited - such as Ohio, for example, where a limit of $40,000 applies. The allowance may be paid as a lump sum or in periodic installments.

You will need to check the laws of your state to determine the precise level of allowance which is applicable to the deceased's estate.

Important Note

If a surviving spouse or child wishes to claim the family allowance, he or she may be required under state law do so in writing within a specific time frame. In addition, he or she may need to survive the deceased spouse/ parent by a specific number of days depending on state law.

The Exemption for the Benefit of the Family

In addition to the above rights, a spouse is entitled in certain states to certain property of the deceased spouse (subject to certain monitory limitations) irrespective of whether the deceased's will provides to the contrary. That property is legally considered not to be part of the probate estate, where there is a will, or the intestate estate where there is no will.

In states that have adopted the Uniform Probate Code, the property to which the spouse is entitled includes household furniture, automobiles, furnishings, appliances and personal effects not exceeding $10,000 in value. If any of the property selected is encumbered and the value in excess of security interests, plus that of other exempt property, is less than $10,000, or if there is not $10,000 worth of exempt property in the estate, the spouse or children are entitled to other assets of the estate, if any, to the extent necessary to make up the $10,000 value. Rights to exempt property and assets needed to make up a deficiency of exempt property have priority over all claims against the estate, but the right to any assets to make up a deficiency of exempt property abates as necessary to permit earlier payment of homestead allowance and family allowance. These rights are in addition to any benefit or share passing to the surviving spouse or children by the deceased's will, unless otherwise provided, by intestate succession, or by way of elective share.

If there is no surviving spouse, the deceased's children are entitled jointly to the same value.

Important Note

If a surviving spouse or child wishes to claim this exemption, he or she may be required under state law do so in writing within a specific time frame. In addition, he or she may need to survive the deceased spouse/parent by a specific number of days depending on state law.

Right to Remain in the Family Home

A surviving spouse will generally have the right to remain in the family home, if it is a probate asset, for a period of up to one year from the date of death of the deceased. In some states, this period is extended to a right to remain in the family residence for life. This is so notwithstanding that the house may have been gifted to someone else under the terms of the deceased's will. Where the family home is sold to pay debts of the estate during this period of time, a surviving spouse may be entitled to receive an amount from the estate equal to the fair rental value of the property.

The election to exercise the right to remain in the family home must be exercised within a specific time frame following the initial appointment of an executor or else the right lapses. You will need to check the specific period of time which applies in the deceased's former state of residence.

Right to Receive Family Residence

In certain states, depending upon the value of the property, a surviving spouse may have the right to receive the family residence as part of his or her inheritance.

A surviving spouse may also have the right to purchase certain assets of the probate estate at the appraised values. Where this is intended, an application or petition to purchase the assets must be filed within the required time frames as set out under state law. These time frames usually coincide with the filing on the inventory by the executor.

Right to Automobiles

In certain states, the surviving spouse and/or children of the deceased may be entitled to receive automobiles from the estate notwithstanding they were not left to the them under the deceased's will. In some cases, these assets fall under the entitlement referred to above as being for the benefit of the family. Again, where applicable, this right should be exercised within the specific time frame set out under state law. This time frame typically ties in with the initial appointment of the executor. As with the other rights of election above, the right is forfeited if not exercised within the prescribed time frame.

Right to Reimbursement of Funeral Bill

In some states, a spouse is also entitled to be reimbursed by the deceased's estate for the payment of the deceased's funeral bill.

Abatement of Assets

As mentioned earlier, high levels of debt or the lack of cash within an estate can create a situation where assets need to be sold in order to pay these debts. This process is known as abatement. The sale of assets in this manner can result in you being unable to make certain bequests to people specified in the will.

If a situation arises where assets need to be abated in this manner, you may wish to call a meeting of the beneficiaries, especially the primary ones, to advise them of the situation. There is of course no obligation to do this. However, it sometimes makes sense to explain to the beneficiaries the changes that may need to be made to the bequests set out in the will and why those changes are being made.

Disclaimed Inheritances

A beneficiary can renounce or disclaim their entitlement to receive a gift under the will in favor of an alternate beneficiary specified to receive that gift. If no alternate beneficiary is named, the gift will be passed to the beneficiary or beneficiaries entitled to the residue of the estate.

A gift may be disclaimed for several reasons - because it's unwanted, carries heavy liabilities (property maintenance, for example), tax reasons, or because the intended beneficiary simply wants to pass the gift to another beneficiary.

Beneficiaries who wish to disclaim a gift must notify you as soon as possible as there are specific time frames within which they must disclaim the gift. These time limits vary from state to state. For federal estate tax purposes, the disclaimer must be in writing and must be filed within 9 months following the date of death of the testator.

Did You Know?

"Final settlement" is the executor's last job!

Petitioning the Court to Approve the Plan of Distribution

Once you have prepared your accounting and plan of distribution, the next step is usually to petition the court to convene a hearing for the purpose of approving the plan – although this is not required in every state. You should check the precise requirements in the state in which the probate is being carried out.

This petition typically includes the following parts:

- an accounting (unless you have received signed waivers from the interested persons waiving their right to an accounting - see above);
- a report of the administration. This report consists of a summary of the steps you took as executor in administering the estate; and
- a petition requesting the court to approve the accounting (if filed), the distribution of the estate assets and any additional matters that require court approval (such as, for example, the payment of fees to you as executor or to the estate attorney).

Sample Form

Sample Petition for Final Settlement and Distribution - State of Colorado

<table>
<tr><td>□ District Court □ Denver Probate Court

______________________________County, Colorado
Court Address:

IN THE MATTER OF THE ESTATE OF:

Deceased:

Attorney or Party Without Attorney (Name and Address):

Phone Number: E-mail:
FAX Number: Atty. Reg. #:</td><td>COURT USE ONLY

Case Number:

Division:
Courtroom:</td></tr>
<tr><td colspan="2">PETITION FOR FINAL SETTLEMENT AND DISTRIBUTION</td></tr>
</table>

1. Petitioner, as the personal representative of this estate, has collected and managed the assets, filed the inventory and accounting and performed all other acts required of petitioner by law.

2. The time for presenting claims which arose prior to the death of the deceased has expired.

3. The proposed schedule of distribution is attached.

4. □ The court has previously determined testacy and heirs following lawful notice to all interested persons.

   □ The Registrar has previously informally admitted to

probate the deceased's will and petitioner affirms the statements in the application for informal probate and appointment of personal representative.

□ Petitioner affirms the statements in the application for informal appointment as personal representative of an intestate estate.

5. □ Other:____

____

____

PETITIONER REQUESTS that the court set a time and place of hearing; that notice be given to all interested persons as provided by law; that after notice and hearing, the court determine testacy and heirs if not previously determined; determine the persons entitled to distribution; accept the final accounting as presented; direct the personal representative to distribute the remaining assets of the estate; and upon filing final receipts or evidence of distribution, discharge the personal representative and any surety on the personal representative's bond.

Date: ______________________

____

Signature of attorney for petitioner

Signature of Petitioner

(Type or Print name, address, & tele. # below)

____

____

____

Where the probate is being carried out in states that have adopted the Uniform Probate Code and in various other states, you will need to notify all interested persons of the hearing.

Where no objection is raised to the accounting or plan within the time frame set out under state law (usually 30 to 60 days), you are free to distribute the assets in accordance with your plan of distribution. If an objection is raised, the court will consider it, make any changes to the distribution plan it deems appropriate and issue an order that you distribute the assets as determined by the court.

Task Checklist

Are You Ready to Close the Probate Estate?

- Have you published a Probate Notice to Creditors and allowed the relevant time for creditors' claims to lapse?
- Have you received any valid Creditor's Claims? If so have they been agreed and paid?
- Have you discharged all relevant taxes?
- If you are seeking remuneration for your services, have you determined the amount of that fee?
- If you engaged attorneys, appraisers or accountants on behalf of the estate, have you determined and agreed the fees paid or to be paid to them?
- If you have completed ALL of the above, you are ready to close the estate.

Giving Notice of the Hearing

In order to give notice of the hearing, you will need to complete an appropriate Notice of Hearing form (see sample on the ensuing pages) and have someone mail or personally deliver it to each person who is entitled to receive notice. In most cases, you cannot mail or deliver the papers yourself. As such, you should arrange for someone else to do the actual mailing or delivery for you. Once they have done this, you will need to have them sign a standard declaration of service (see sample on the snsuing pages). The Notice of Hearing should be delivered to the interested parties within the required timeframe set out under state law, usually 15 days or so before the hearing date. In most cases, all you will need to send is the Notice of Hearing. It can however be helpful to include a copy of the petition.

Notice must be given to all interested persons (see Chapter 8 for details on interested persons).

Finally, you will need to file the original Notice of Hearing with the completed Certificate of Service by Mail with the probate filing clerk.

Sample Form

<table>
<tr><th colspan="2">Sample Notice of hearing on petition for final settlement and distribution - State of Colorado</th></tr>
<tr><td>□ District court □ Denver probate court

________________________________County, Colorado
court Address:

IN THE MATTER OF THE Estate OF:

Deceased:

Attorney or Party Without Attorney
(Name and Address):

Phone Number: E-mail:
FAX Number: Atty. Reg.#:</td><td>COURT USE ONLY

Case Number:

Division:
Courtroom:</td></tr>
<tr><td colspan="2">NOTICE OF HEARING ON PETITION FOR FINAL SETTLEMENT AND DISTRIBUTION</td></tr>
</table>

TO ALL INTERESTED PERSONS:

A hearing on the Petition for Final Settlement and Distribution, a copy of which is attached to this Notice, will be held at the following time and location or at a later date to which the hearing may be continued.

Date and Time: ______________________________
Courtroom or Division:________________________
Address:_________________________________

Interested persons have the responsibility to protect their own rights and interests within the time and in the manner provided by the Colorado Probate Code, including the appropriateness of claims paid, the compensation of personal representatives, attorneys and others and the distribution of estate assets. The court will not review or adjudicate these or other matters unless specifically requested to do so by an interested person. If any interested person desires to object, such person shall file specific written objections and shall furnish the personal representative with a copy at or before the hearing.

Attendance at this hearing is not mandatory. Actual distribution of estate assets normally does not occur at the hearing.

____

Signature of Petitioner or Attorney for Petitioner Date

____
____
____
____

Type or Print name, address & tele. # of Petitioner

NOTE: This form or CPC24-NA must be used in formal proceedings terminating an estate. (Section 15-12-1001 or 1002, C.R.S. and Rule 8.3, C.R.P.P.) Use of this form is limited to an appearance hearing.

CERTIFICATE OF SERVICE

I certify that on (date) ______________________________, a copy of this Notice of Hearing on Petition for Final Settlement and Distribution was served on each of the following at the indicated address by:

□ hand delivery □ certified U.S. mail, postage pre-paid
□ first class U.S. mail, postage pre-paid

□ registered U.S. mail, postage pre-paid

Name and Address

____

Signature of Person Certifying Service

NOTE: This certificate of service cannot be used in cases where personal service is required or used. Use CPC7-P (Personal Service Affidavit) or CPC8-A (Waiver of Service) for each person required to be served personally.

Distributing the Estate Assets

While the law varies from state to state the general rule of good practice (and indeed the rule of law in many cases) is that all the assets should not be paid out or transferred to the beneficiaries until the court has approved the executor's filings regarding assets, claims, taxes, etc. This general rule does not, in many states, apply in respect of the payment of certain allowances, such as the family allowance, which are designed to alleviate some of the financial hardship which may exist for the deceased's family. As such, a portion of the assets can be paid out by way of partial distributions before the final distribution.

In order to transfer specific assets to the beneficiaries, you will need to evaluate the legal and procedural requirements applicable to the transfer of those assets. We have examined the transfer procedures associated with some of the more commonly held assets below.

Real Estate

Real estate is transferred to the beneficiary by recording details of the transfer on the court order for final settlement and distribution. Usually, no other deed is required. Once the order has issued, it will need to be filed in the registry of deeds in which the property is located.

Cars, Boats and Other Vehicles

In a number of states, one or more vehicles (in some cases up to a certain value only) can be transferred to the deceased's surviving spouse outside of the probate process. The transfer is achieved by having the surviving spouse complete a written declaration known as an affidavit. The affidavit sets out details of the vehicle being transferred.

Where the surviving spouse is unable to avail of the non-probate transfer provisions referred to above or where the vehicle is left to a different beneficiary, they will need to complete the required state specific form in order to register the transfer of the vehicle. Some states also charge tax on this transfer document. You should check with the department of motor vehicles to determine the specific transfer requirements which apply in the state in which the vehicle is registered. Also, if the deceased has a boat which has been registered with the Coast Guard (although very few are), you will need to check with them to determine what their specific transfer requirements are.

Cash Accounts

Cash gifts, or pecuniary legacies as they are also called, can be made by simply writing a check drawn on the estate bank account in favor of the beneficiary. However, it's often more practical to use some means by which the funds are extracted from the estate bank account immediately – such as a bank draft – as this will allow you to close the bank account without having to wait for a number of days, weeks or even months for the beneficiary to cash the check.

Where checks are used, it's common practice to have the beneficiary sign an acknowledgement on the back of the check to the effect that he or she acknowledges receipt of the funds in satisfaction of a certain gift payable under the will. Once the check has been lodged by the beneficiary and cashed, the bank will return the cashed check to you as a cancelled check. This cancelled check will then act as a receipt in the absence of having a formal receipt (see below). You should note however that not all banks provide this return service. Where they do not, we recommend that you get the beneficiary to sign some form of acknowledgement that he or she received the funds.

United States Savings Bonds

You will need to contact the deceased's bank to obtain the appropriate form as well as details of the procedure involved in transferring the bonds to a beneficiary. Once the transfer is completed, the bonds will be re-issued in the name of the beneficiary. You will need to complete a Treasury Form PD 1455 and send the completed form back with a copy of your letters of authority, a copy of the deceased's death certificate and any certificate of title evidencing the bonds.

Broker Accounts

It's also possible to transfer a broker account held with a brokerage firm or with a mutual fund company directly to a beneficiary. You will however need to contact the firm/company to determine whether they can simply change the name on the account or whether they will have to close the existing account and open a new one in the name of the beneficiary. Again, you will most likely need to send a copy of your letters of authority and a copy of the deceased's death certificate.

Publicly Quoted Stocks and Bonds

To transfer stocks to a beneficiary, you will need to contact the company's share registrar (or transfer agent as it's often called) and request that they be transferred to and re-issued in the name of the beneficiary. The sock certificate issued in the deceased's name should indicate the name of the transfer agent. If not, the details should be obtainable directly from the quoted company. Once you determine who the agent is, you will most likely need to send the following documents to them (but call and check what documents they need before you send anything!) in order to have the stock re-issued in the name of the beneficiary:-

- the original stock certificate relating to the quoted company in question;
- a letter of instruction from you, which is signature guaranteed by a bank,

trust company or a brokerage firm registered with the New York Stock Exchange;

- a stock power of attorney, which again is signature guaranteed in the manner described above;
- a copy of your letters of authority; and
- a copy of the deceased's death certificate.

Instead of sending the above items to the transfer agent, you could always send the above documents to a broker with instructions that they open an account in the name of the beneficiary and then have the stocks in question re-issued 'in street name' in the brokerage account. Of course, the stock can be reissued in the name of the beneficiary if you or the beneficiary wish but street accounts are easy to deal with.

Did You Know?

What does "in street name" mean?

A brokerage account where the customer's securities and assets are held under the name of the brokerage firm, rather than the name of the individual who purchased the security or asset; are said to be held in 'street name'.

If you want to transfer municipal and corporate bonds to a beneficiary, you can do so in a similar manner to quoted stock.

You should be aware that as bearer bonds, which are unregistered, are payable to the bearer or physical holder of the bonds, there are no formal transfer procedures.

Other Property

If you want to transfer any other property to a beneficiary, a simple deed of assignment should suffice. However, if there are specific documents required to effect transfers of property (such as share transfer forms for a corporation) then you should use the required form. If you are uncertain as to how to proceed, we suggest that you contact an attorney.

Transfer of Joint Tenancy, Community and Other Survivorship Property

As the transfer of joint tenancy, community property and other survivorship property takes place outside probate, an executor will not ordinarily have authority or responsibility to deal these matters. However, in practice, executors may often be surviving spouses or may have been joint owners of property with the deceased. As such, it's useful to touch on the topic in passing at least.

In the case of real estate at least, the manner in which a surviving joint owner transfers title in the deceased's share of a property into his or her sole name is similar in most states. In essence, he or she will need to file a document with the land registry indicating that the deceased has passed away and that, as a result, he or she is now the sole owner of the property. Of course, if there are other surviving owners, the property will be transferred to their names collectively. In some states, it suffices to simply file a copy of the deceased's death certificate in the land registry. With that, the land registry will record the change in ownership of the property. However, in other states, it's necessary for the surviving joint owner to sign an affidavit (a sworn statement) confirming that he or she is the surviving joint owner and requesting that the title to the property be transferred into his or her name. We recommend that you check with the local land registry to determine the precise requirements which apply.

Distributing Property to Children

Depending on state's laws, minor children may only receive a nominal amount of property in to their own names under the terms of a will. The amount varies between approximately $1,000 and $5,000 depending on the state in question. If the deceased left a gift to a minor in excess of the permitted statutory amount, it will not be possible to transfer that gift to the minor directly. Instead, you will have to transfer it to the child's legal guardian or trustee as named under the deceased's will. If the deceased did not appoint a guardian or trustee, the court will do it by appointing someone to serve as the children's "property guardian". A court will often appoint the surviving parent but this is not always the case. A third party or court appointed guardian can be appointed to deal with the property and, in such cases, that property guardian will have complete control over the minor's inheritance.

Obtaining and Filing Receipts

In advance of an executor being discharged from the office of executor, he or she must demonstrate that the estate has been distributed to the rightful beneficiaries. The executor demonstrates this by providing written receipts to the court. It is therefore vital that you obtain a signed receipt from all persons receiving property from the estate. It may even be wise to hold back on transferring a gift to a beneficiary unless they simultaneously sign a receipt. A sample form of a receipt is set out on the next page and should be required from each beneficiary. However, you should be aware that many states have formal receipts which must be completed by the beneficiary and produced to the court. As such, you will need to check the laws in the state in which the probate is being administered. Each receipt should be filed with the court prior to filing a petition for final discharge.

Sample Form

<table>
<tr><th colspan="2">Sample Receipt and Release - State of California</th></tr>
<tr><td>□ District Court □ Denver Probate Court

________________________________ County, Colorado
Court Address:

□ In the Interests of:
□ In the Matter of the Estate of:

Attorney or Party Without Attorney (Name and Address):

Phone Number: E-mail:
FAX Number: Atty. Reg. #:</td><td>COURT USE ONLY

Case Number:

Division:
Courtroom:</td></tr>
<tr><th colspan="2">RECEIPT AND RELEASE</th></tr>
</table>

Received from ____,

□Personal Representative

□Conservator

□ Partial

□ Full payment and satisfaction of the following:

□ the devise to me in the will under article(s) ______________

______________________________________.

□ my ________ share of the estate in the will under article(s)

____________________________________.

□ my ________ share of the estate as heir.

□ my distribution from the conservatorship case.

□ Cash in the amount of $ ___________________.

□ Tangible personal property described as: * _______________________________

____

____

The following securities: * ____

____

____

□ Other (describe): * ____

____

____

□ I grant a partial release and satisfaction to the fiduciary of the estate as to the above partial distribution.

□ I grant a full and final release and satisfaction to the estate and to the fiduciary and his or her successors for any liability in connection with my interest in the estate.

Date: _______________________________

Signature: _______________________________

(Type or print name below)

* Attach additional sheets as necessary.

Closing the Estate

Once you are satisfied that you have accounted for and distributed the deceased's estate in full, you can seek to end your appointment as executor. Ordinarily, this is done through informal proceedings rather than formal proceedings. With informal proceedings, you simply file a statement with the court indicating that you have done everything required of you as executor. You will need to mail a copy of this statement to all interested persons. Depending on the law of the state in which the probate is being carried out, a particular period of time will need to have elapsed following the opening of the estate before you can file for an informal closing in this manner. Under the Uniform

Probate Code, the required period is six months; however, in non Uniform Probate Code states, the period does vary. If anyone objects to the closing of the estate, they may seek a formal hearing in court to address any outstanding issues or problems. If no objection is filed within the time frame set out under state law, your obligations as executor will end one year from date of the filing.

Sample Form

<table>
<tr><th colspan="2">Sample Statement for Informal Closing - State of Colorado</th></tr>
<tr><td>□ District court □ Denver probate court

________________________ County, Colorado
Court Address:

IN THE MATTER OF THE ESTATE OF:

Deceased

Attorney or Party Without Attorney (Name and Address):

Phone Number: E-mail:
FAX Number: Atty. Reg. #:</td><td>COURT USE ONLY

Case Number:

Division:
Courtroom:</td></tr>
<tr><th colspan="2">VERIFIED STATEMENT OF PERSONAL REPRESENTATIVE CLOSING ADMINISTRATION</th></tr>
</table>

The undersigned personal representative of this estate states:

1. Six months have passed since the original appointment of a general personal representative for this estate or at least one year has passed since the deceased's death. The date of the original appointment was ________________________.

2. Except as may be disclosed on an attached explanation, the undersigned or a preceding personal representative has fully administered this estate by making payment, settlement or other disposition of: all lawful claims; expenses of

administration; federal and state estate taxes, inheritance taxes and other death taxes; and the deceased's estate's federal and state income taxes. The assets of the estate have been distributed to the persons entitled to receive such assets in the amount and in the manner to which they were entitled. If any claims are listed on an attached explanation as remaining undischarged, an explanation of arrangements for their disposition is also listed.

3. The undersigned has sent a copy of this statement to all distributees of this estate and to all creditors or other claimants whose claims are neither paid nor barred and has furnished a full account in writing of the undersigned's administration to the distributees whose interests are affected.

4. No court order prohibits the informal closing of this estate. Administration of this estate is not supervised.

This statement is filed for the purpose of closing this estate. The appointment of the personal representative will terminate one year after this statement is filed with the court if no proceedings involving the undersigned are then pending. (§ 15-12-1003, C.R.S.)

As the personal representative and being sworn, I verify that the facts set forth in this statement are true to the best of my knowledge, information and belief.
DATE:____

____

Signature of Personal Representative
(Type or Print name, address & telephone # below)

____

____

state of ____
County of____

Subscribed and sworn to before me by the personal
representative on : ________________________

My commission expires ____________________________

Notary Public/(Deputy) Clerk of court

CERTIFICATE OF SERVICE

I certify that on (date) ________________________________, a copy of this Verified statement of Personal Representative Closing

Administration was served on each of the following at the indicated address by:

□ hand delivery □ certified U.S. mail, postage pre-paid

□ first class U.S. mail, postage pre-paid □ registered U.S. mail, postage pre-paid

Name and Address

____

____

____

____

Signature of Person Certifying Service

NOTE: This certificate of service cannot be used in cases where personal service is required or used. Use CPC7-P (Personal Service Affidavit) or CPC8-A (Waiver of Service) for each person required to be served personally

Alternatively, you can formally close the estate by convening a final hearing at which you will petition the court to expedite the termination of your duties as executor. In most states, you can do this at any time provided of course that the applicable period within which creditors can file claims against the estate has lapsed. Again, notice of the hearing must be provided to all interested persons. At the hearing, if the judge accepts that you have properly administered the office of executor and done everything that you ought to have done, then an order of court will be issued closing the estate and determining your duties on such date as falls 30 days (usually) after the date of the order. The 30 day time frame is the time allowed to appeal the judge's order. As you will appreciate, given the additional expenses associated with a formal hearing, it is seldom used unless potential litigation makes it useful or necessary.

Once the probate has closed and your role as executor has come to an end, you will cease to have authority to deal with estate assets. As such, if assets are discovered after this time, the beneficiaries will need to petition the court to re-open the estate. This petition will also provide for the appointment of an executor. This may or may not be you. Each state has specific forms and procedures applicable to the re-opening of an estate so check the precise requirements with the local probate court.

What If the Estate Isn't Ready to Be Closed?

Generally, executors are required to file a petition for final distribution or a verified report on the status of the estate within one year after they have been officially appointed as executor. This one year period can increase to 18 months where a federal estate tax return is required to be made. The status report should indicate the condition of the estate, the specific reasons why it cannot be closed and distributed (e.g. ongoing litigation, tax audits, assets need to be sold, etc) and also the estimated time needed to close the estate.

A hearing will be convened in the same manner as other probate hearing in order to receive and consider the status report. Again, all interested persons have an entitlement to receive notice of the hearing. At the hearing itself, the court will consider the reasons for the delay in closing and will make any order it feels appropriate to expedite the closing.

If an executor fails to file a status report, any interested person may petition the court to have the executor file the report. More importantly, for you, if this occurs the court may reduce the level of compensation payable to you as executor of the estate or even terminate your appointment as executor.

CHAPTER 12:
THE SETTLING OF TRUSTS

Chapter Overview

While the task of settling a living trust is very similar to that of probating an estate, it's useful to touch on this area specifically as many executors often find themselves acting as both executor of somebody's estate and successor trustee of their living trust. So, in this chapter, we'll take a quick look at living trusts and the main tasks involved in winding them up.

CHAPTER 12

THE SETTLING OF TRUSTS

What Is a Trust?

A trust can be described as a fiduciary arrangement whereby one or more persons become the legal owners of trust property, which they hold not on their own behalf but for the use and benefit of somebody else.

Did You Know?

A trust is a legal entity or device established by a person, usually under written agreement, and used to manage real or personal property for the benefit of another.

Every trust has a number of core components. These include:-

(i) the grantor (also called a settlor, donor or creator) - the person who sets up the trust;

(ii) the objective of the trust – why it has been set up;

(iii) the trust property – the property which has been placed into the trust;

(iv) the trustee – the person who will manage the trust property;

(v) the beneficiaries – the people entitled to receive the trust property; and

(vi) the rules of the trust.

These 'core elements' must be contained in every trust. Usually, the terms of the trust are set out in either a deed or a will, which in the case of a deed or declaration is created by the grantor or, in the case of a will, by the testator.

Under the terms of a trust, a grantor 'settles' trust property on one or more trustees for the benefit of one or more beneficiaries. The trustee, in turn, assumes an obligation to preserve and protect the trust property and generally manage the trust's affairs on behalf of the beneficiaries.

The standard of care that a trustee must observe in carrying out his or her obligation is one of the highest known to the law. A trustee must always act for the benefit of and in the best interests of the beneficiaries of the trust and never for his or her own personal gain. The trustee must also exercise due care and diligence in the management of the trust property. The obligation of the trustee extends to vesting or transferring the trust property to the beneficiaries upon the happening of a future event (e.g. when they attain a specific age, complete college or satisfy whatever conditions are set out in the trust).

A trustee will have the similar fiduciary duties as those outlined for executors in Chapter 2.

Trust property can be any form of property, including cash, real estate and every type of personal property. The trust deed (or the will) basically just says what the trustee can do, can't do and must do. It may also define who can be a beneficiary and who can't.

What Exactly Are Living Trusts?

A living trust is a trust which is created for the simple purpose of holding ownership of the grantor's assets outside of the grantor's probatable estate during his or her lifetime and, following his or her death, distributing those assets to named beneficiaries. By holding ownership of the assets outside of the grantor's estate in this manner, the assets will fall outside of the probate net. Because the assets will not be tied up in probate following the grantor's death, they can be quickly distributed to the beneficiaries of the trust.

A revocable living trust is created by simply executing an agreement (or deed) pursuant to which a trustee agrees to hold and manage certain trust property on behalf of the grantor. One of the unique features of revocable living trusts however is that the same person will, in the majority of cases, act as both grantor and trustee. By also playing the role of trustee, the grantor can maintain control over and use of the assets he or she transfers to the trust.

As living trusts are ordinarily revocable, the grantor reserves the right to revoke or terminate the trust and resume personal ownership of the trust property at any time. In addition, the grantor also maintains the right, exercisable at his or her discretion, to add to or withdraw assets from the trust property, to change the terms of the trust and even to make it irrevocable at some time in the future.

After the grantor (or the grantor and his/her spouse in the case of a joint living trust) dies, a person known as a successor trustee (like an executor in many respects) will step to manage the trust property and to distribute it to the beneficiaries named in the trust deed. The successor trustee is usually named in the trust deed.

In most cases, the distribution of the trust assets by the successor trustee takes only a few weeks because it all takes place outside of probate and away from the supervision of the court! The living trust ceases to exist when all of the trust property has been transferred to the beneficiaries.

Parties to a Living Trust

While the parties to a living trust are pretty much the same as those which are party to a normal trust, its worth having a quick look at them at this juncture so that you can familiarize yourself with same.

The principal parties are as follows:-

Grantor/Settlor	This is the person who sets up the trust.
Trustee	This is the person who will manage the trust property. When it comes to revocable living trusts, the grantor usually acts as trustee.
Successor Trustee	The successor trustee is the person who will step up to manage the trust property when the grantor dies or in the event that the grantor becomes incapacitated. When the grantor dies, the successor trustee will distribute the assets in the trust in accordance with the terms of the living trust agreement/deed. He or she will not have any power to amend the terms of the trust agreement/deed. Separately, should the grantor become incapacitated, the successor will take up management of the trust assets in accordance with the terms of the trust agreement/deed.
Beneficiaries	These are the people who are entitled to receive the benefit of the trust's assets upon the grantor's death.

The Successor Trustee

As mentioned, the successor trustee is the person who assumes control of the trust after the grantor (as initial trustee) becomes incapacitated and/or dies. Once the successor trustee assumes control of the trust, he or she will be obliged to manage and deal with the trust assets in accordance with the terms of the trust agreement. In the case of the grantor's death, the successor trustee will also be responsible for transferring ownership of the trust assets to the beneficiaries named in the trust agreement.

In the case of a shared or joint trust (where there is more than one grantor), the successor trustee will take over control of the trust when both trustees are incapacitated or dead. The successor trustee will have no authority to act while any of the grantors remain alive or capable of managing the trust.

The trust agreement will identify the person or persons who will act as successor trustee(s) of the trust. In most cases, this is usually a relative or a family friend or the executor of the grantor's estate.

Similar to the position with executors, it is important to note that even where you are named in a trust agreement to act as successor trustee, you are under absolutely no obligation to carry out the role and cannot be forced to do so. You are perfectly entitled to decline to act. Where this happens, the next named successor trustee will take over the management and administration of the trust. If no alternate is named or none of the named alternates are willing to serve, the beneficiaries of the trust will need to petition the local court to appoint someone to fill the role.

Once a person takes on the role, they may choose to resign. However, in the normal course, they cannot be replaced or relieved until a new successor trustee takes over. This is to ensure that the trust is not left unmanaged at any time.

What Must the Successor Trustee Do When the Grantor Dies?

When the grantor dies, it will be the successor trustee's responsibility to assume control of the trust estate and administer it in accordance with the terms of the living trust agreement. In much the same way as the deceased's estate is administered for probate, the administration process for trusts involves the collection of assets, payment of debts and taxes and the distribution of assets to the ultimate beneficiaries of the living trust. In the majority of cases these beneficiaries are the grantor's spouse and/or children; however a grantor may pass his or her trust assets to virtually anyone. Of course, spouses have certain rights so if the grantor is married his or her freedom will be restricted as outlined in previous chapters.

In any event, let's take a brief look at what's generally involved in the 'administration' process.

Obtain Certified Copies of the Death Certificate

Similar to the administration of the probate estates, one of the successor trustee's first tasks following the death of the grantor will be to procure copies of the grantor's death certificate. This certificate, together with an affidavit of trust, will need to be presented to third parties in order to establish that the successor trustee is lawfully entitled to deal with the trust assets. For example, financial institutions such as banks and life insurance companies will ordinarily require these documents before allowing the successor trustee to access any accounts or policies in the trust's name.

A death certificate can generally be obtained from the state Office of Vital Records or from the Department of Health, but there are some variations from state to state. The successor trustee could also contact the grantor's general practitioner or funeral director each of whom should be able to procure a copy of the death certificate.

Obtain a Tax Identification Number for the Trust

Next, the successor trustee will need to make an application to the IRS in order to obtain a tax identification number for the trust. The application can be made using the IRS Form 1041.

In the case of a shared living trust (where there is more than one grantors), an application may need to be made for a tax number of each of the two resulting trusts. The first trust, being the trust of the deceased spouse, will need a new tax number regardless as it has become irrevocable. Whether or not the second trust created for the surviving spouse requires a new tax identification number depends on the nature of the trust in question. If the successor trustee is a surviving spouse and no AB trust (a type of living trust for a couple) is created, the successor trustee may use his or her social security number, as the tax identification number for the second trust. If, however, an AB trust is created, a new tax identification number will be required for the second trust also.

Notify Beneficiaries

When the grantor dies, the successor trustee is obliged to notify all the potential beneficiaries of the grantor's death and of their possible entitlements under the terms of the trust document. This obligation to notify beneficiaries can be contained within the terms of the trust document or enshrined in state legislation itself.

For example, section 7-303 of the Probate Code provides that:

> "the trustee shall keep the beneficiaries of the trust reasonably informed of the trust and its administration. In addition:
>
> (a) Within 30 days after his acceptance of the trust, the trustee shall inform in writing the current beneficiaries...........of the Court in which the trust is registered and of his name and address.
>
> (b) Upon reasonable request, the trustee shall provide the beneficiary with a copy of the terms of the trust which describe or affect his interest and with relevant information about the assets of the trust and the particulars relating to the administration.
>
> (c) Upon reasonable request, a beneficiary is entitled to a statement of the accounts of the trust annually and on termination of the trust or change of the trustee."

As can be seen from (c) above, the successor trustee is not obligated to deliver a set of trust accounts to a trust beneficiary unless that beneficiary has actually requested a copy of same. The lack of a formal obligation to deliver accounts here is intended to avoid extensive administration burdens on the successor trustee's part while at the same time provide the beneficiary with adequate protection and sources of information. In most cases, where a request is made for an accounting, the successor trustee will send the beneficiary a copy of the annual tax returns together with a narrative explaining the movements of trust assets and funds.

Collection and Management of Trust Assets

Having obtained a death certificate and made an affidavit of trust, the next task for the successor trustee will be to take possession of the trust's assets and to evaluate what debts, claims, taxes and other expenses will be payable by the trust. The successor trustee should work very closely with the executor of the grantor's estate in order to determine what assets have been transferred into the trust.

The successor trustee should commence the process by reviewing the trust agreement and trust records in order to establish what assets have been transferred into the trust and what debts might exist. In this respect, the successor trustee should review the schedule of trust assets at the back of the trust agreement/deed (if there is such a schedule) and carefully review any title deeds and certificates which are located amongst the grantor's possessions. Title deeds tend to give a clear indication as to whether assets have been transferred to the trust or not.

The successor trustee should, working in conjunction with the executor, carry out a full search for assets which may belong to the trust. This search will be done in pretty much the same way as outlined in previous chapters for executors. The successor trustee will need to review the deceased grantor's records, contact financial institutions, contact the grantor's advisors and so on.

Once the successor actually locates trust assets he will need to secure them in the same way as an executor should. Securities (especially bearer bonds), title deeds, jewelry and other items of substantial value should be placed in a safe deposit box or safe. It's also important to ensure that the trust assets (including real estate) are adequately insured against risks such as fire, damage, theft, loss and liability, as appropriate. To this end, the successor trustee will need to contact the insurance companies to ensure that the death of the grantor has not caused the termination of any of the existing policies. If any of these policies have been terminated or where no policy was previously in existence to cover some or all of the trust assets, the successor trustee should organize appropriate cover.

Once the available assets are secured, the successor trustee should proceed to obtain a valuation of those assets and to actually collect the trust assets.

Claim Life Insurance Proceeds

The successor trustee should contact any insurance company with whom the grantor held a policy of life insurance. If the living trust was named as a designated beneficiary on that policy the successor should make a claim for any insurance proceeds due to the trust. As mentioned above, the insurance company will require copies of the death certificate and an affidavit of trust. In addition, it will require the successor trustee to fill out standard claim forms. Once the claim has been processed, the funds should be paid to the trust.

Once the insurance proceeds are paid out, they should be transferred into a federally insured trust account pending subsequent release to the beneficiaries.

Gain Access to Bank Accounts and Other Financial Accounts

Each financial institution which held an account for the trust should be notified of the death of the grantor so that it can commence the process of releasing the proceeds of the accounts to the trust. Again, similar to insurance companies above, the financial institutions will require copies of the death certificate and an affidavit of trust from the successor trustee. Similar to the case in respect of insurance proceeds, once the funds are released the proceeds should be transferred into a federally insured trust account.

Identify Debts Owed By the Grantor

A detailed examination of the grantor's affairs will need to be carried out in order to determine what debts may be due and owing by the trust. In this respect, the successor trustee should liaise closely with the executor of the grantor's estate to identify any such debts as the executor also needs to carry out a thorough review of the grantor's affairs.

In the ordinary course, and unless the trust agreement says otherwise, there is no obligation on the successor trustee to use any of the trust assets to discharge debts owing by the grantor personally (as opposed to debts owing by the trust which must be paid from the trust's assets). It will be the responsibility of the executor of the grantor's estate to discharge those deaths from the grantor's probatable assets.

Management of the Trust Assets

Similar to the executor, in order to protect the value of the trust estate, the successor trustee will need to reduce unnecessary outgoings, deal with depreciating assets, manage real estate, manage investments, discharge debts, and so on. The successor trustee will need to take appropriate actions to ensure that the value of the trust estate is maintained. In addition, the successor trustee may need to sell some of the trust assets to pay debts or to facilitate the proper distribution of the trust estate – particularly where the residuary trust estate is divided amongst several beneficiaries in percentages or fractions.

For further discussion on the management of assets, see Chapter 6.

Maintain Proper Accountings of Trust Assets

A trustee will be under a duty to prepare an annual accounting in respect of the trust assets, unless the beneficiaries waive their rights to this or the trust agreement provides otherwise. The accounting should display details of the assets held by the trust at the date of death of the grantor and their current market valuations. The accounting should also include details of any income received, any expenditure made and any assets added to or taken out of the trust.

It's worth reiterating the point that, like an executor, the successor trustee should keep meticulous records of all disbursements from the trust. To this end, we would recommend that money be disbursed in the form of a check so that an audit trail exists of all transactions carried out by the successor trustee on behalf of the trust.

Finally, in order to determine market valuations for some of the trust assets, the successor trustee may need to engage professional valuation agents such as stockbrokers, realtors etc. The preparation of this valuation is important from the point of view of determining what federal estate tax, if any, will be owing by the grantor. As the living trust will be treated as transparent for tax purposes, the successor trustee will need to work closely with the executor of the grantor's estate in order to procure a combined market valuation for all of the grantor's assets at the date of his or her death.

Preparing and Filing Tax Returns

The successor trustee and the executor of the grantor's estate will be collectively responsible for the payment of the various taxes set out below. Payment should first come from the probatable estate and then from the trust estate if the probatable assets are insufficient to discharge the tax liabilities.

Federal Estate Tax

The extent of the grantor's estate both inside and outside the trust will need to be determined. To the extent that the value of that estate exceeds the applicable tax threshold, estate tax will become payable. For details of applicable rates, see chapter 10. It the responsibility of both the successor trustee and the executor to determine if any estate tax is due by the grantor's estate and, if so, to make an appropriate tax return. The successor trustee and executor have a period of nine months from the date of the grantor's death to file the tax return and to discharge any estate taxes that are due. An extension of six month may be obtained in certain circumstances.

Income Taxes

A final income tax return will need to be made for the grantor for the year of his or her death. The return should be made on IRS Form 1040. Again, the payment of tax should be coordinated with the executor.

Trust Income Tax Returns

Following the death of the grantor, all income generated by the living trust will need to be returned separately to the IRS. The return for the trust will be made on IRS Form 1041 for each calendar year. It is the responsibility of the successor trustee to ensure that these returns are made.

Remember, as mentioned above, where the living trust is a shared trust which splits into two separate trusts on the death of the grantor, there will need to be two separate tax returns. The deceased's spouse's trust will file an IRS Form 1041 under its own tax number as outlined in the preceding paragraph. In relation to the trust created for the surviving spouse, if the successor trustee is in fact the surviving spouse and the living trust is not an AB trust, then the successor trustee will file his or her income tax return on an IRS Form 1040. However, if the living trust is an AB trust, the surviving spouse's trust will need to file a Form 1041 under its own tax number.

State Taxes and Pick-Up Taxes

Finally, the successor trustee and executor will also need to discharge any state taxes or pick-up taxes which may be owing by the estate from the overall estate of the grantor.

Transferring Property to Beneficiaries

Once all of the assets have been collected in and all debts and taxes paid or provided for, the successor trustee can distribute the remaining trust assets in accordance with the terms of the living trust. The assets will either be distributed in cash or in kind if the trust includes specific tangible assets.

Of course, in order to properly carry out the distribution, the beneficiaries will need to have the trust assets re-registered in their names by the successor trustee. The successor trustee will need to go through the process for transferring title in the trust assets over to the beneficiaries. After the re-registration is accomplished, the assets are deemed to have been effectively transferred to the beneficiaries of the trust. In each case, the successor trustee should have each beneficiary sign an acknowledgement to confirm that he or she has received the distribution in question.

Administering a Child's Trust

The duties of the successor trustee normally terminate once he or she has distributed the trust assets to the beneficiaries of the trust. However, where the grantor has created a sub-trust for any of his children or indeed any other minor beneficiary named in the living trust, the successor trustee will need to continue acting as trustee of the child's trust. In essence, the successor trustee will need to manage the trust assets left to the child until such time as the child, or children if there is more than one, reaches the age specified in the trust agreement. This will greatly add to the task of the successor trustee as he or she will need to ensure that the trust assets are properly invested and secured for the period of the child's trust as well as make provision from time to time for the welfare, upkeep and education of the child. Only when the last child reaches the age specified in the trust document can the successor trustee formally distribute the remaining assets and wind down the living trust. This may well be years or even decades after the grantor has passed away…..

Conclusion

The length of time that it takes to settle the trust and distribute assets is often dependent on whether an estate tax return is due. If a return will be due, then it is typically prudent to wait until after a closing letter is received from the IRS to make final distributions. This can take 18 months, or more if the estate is audited, after the date of death. However, if no estate tax is due, the trust can usually be wrapped up in a number of months; assuming of course that there are no on-going trusts established under the terms of the living trust itself!

Resource!

For further informatio on living trusts see our book entitle "How to Make a Living Trust & Avoid Probate". See page 290.

INDEX*

A

B

C

D

E

H

I

J

L

O

P

S

U

V

W

Other Great Books from Enodare's Estate Planning Series

Make Your Own Last Will & Testament

By making a will, you can provide for the distribution of your assets to your love ones, appoint guardians to care for your children, provide for the management of gifts to young adults and children, specify how your debts are to be paid following your death, make funeral arrangements and much more.

This book will guide you through the entire process of making a will. It contains all the forms that you will need to make a valid legal will, simply and easily.

Make Your Own Living Trust & Avoid Probate

Living trusts are used to distribute a person's assets after they die in a manner that avoids the costs, delays and publicity of probate. They also cater for the management of property during periods of incapacity.

This book will guide you step-by-step through the process of creating your very own living trust, transferring assets to your living trust and subsequently managing those assets.

All relevant forms are included.

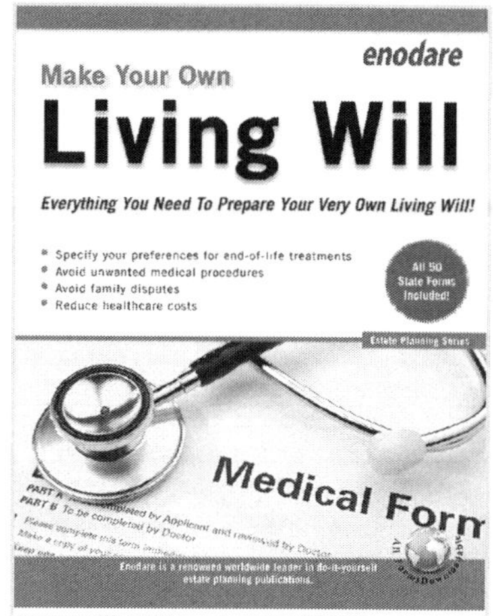

Make Your Own Living Will

Do you want a say in what life sustaining medical treatments you receive during periods in which you are incapacitated and either in a permanent state of unconsciousness or suffering from a terminal illness? Well if so, you must have a living will!

This book will introduce you to living wills, the types of medical procedures that they cover, the matters that you need to consider when making them and, of course, provide you with all the relevant forms you need to make your own living will!

www.enodare.com

8113419R00159

Made in the USA
San Bernardino, CA
28 January 2014